The

COMMUNITY
COLLEGE
PRESIDENCY

at the

MILLENNIUM

◆

George B. Vaughan
and Iris M. Weisman

Foreword by Donald E. Puyear

COMMUNITY COLLEGE PRESS®
a division of the American Association of
Community Colleges
Washington, D.C.

Requests for permission should be sent to
Community College Press
American Association of Community Colleges
One Dupont Circle, NW
Suite 410
Washington, DC 20036
(202) 728-0200

Printed in the United States of America.

ISBN 0-87117-311-5

CONTENTS

Figures

Tables

FOREWORD

George Vaughan and Iris Weisman have provided another important contribution to our understanding of the community college presidency. This is the third national study Vaughan has conducted on the characteristics of community college presidents. The information presented throughout the book will be useful to those who wish to understand community colleges and their leaders. The sections of the work that address both historical and future issues facing community college leaders are intriguing.

The historical perspective of chapter 1 sets the context for a review of personal and professional profiles of today's community college presidents in chapters 2 and 3 ("A Personal Profile of the Presidency" and "A Professional Profile of the Presidency," respectively). These two chapters, and a good bit of chapter 5 ("Women and Minorities in the Community College Presidency"), come from the most recent iteration of Career and Lifestyle Survey (CLS). In this survey, community college presidents were asked a series of questions regarding their personal backgrounds, their education and experience before becoming president, their personal and professional lifestyles as president, and their future plans. As is demonstrated by the type of analysis in these chapters, this research becomes even more valuable when it is repeated over time. Trends are identified and the results of the trends are analyzed.

In chapter 6 ("Establishing and Maintaining Relationships") the human and relational aspects of the presidency are considered. This chapter draws on information on the president-board relationship previously obtained from a complementary study by Vaughan and Weisman.

In-depth interviews with a number of community college presidents are included in a new and quite fascinating feature of this volume. In these interviews, the issues, concerns, and visions of the presidents are explored in a most effective manner. These results are reported in chapter 4 ("Mission and Milieu: Views from the Trenches"), chapter 5 ("Women and Minorities in the Community College Presidency"), and chapter 7 ("Issues Facing Community College Leaders at the Millennium"). These sections are the heart of the work; here one gets the sense of what is really important to today's community college presidents.

Also in chapter 7, the presidents' responses to the survey questions regarding the major issue facing the community college in the next three to four years and what presidents can do to prepare their institutions to face the issue are synthesized. These issues and strategies are followed by comments of the interviewed presidents regarding the leadership skills that will be needed by presidents in the millennium.

Many of the presidents interviewed for this book stated that getting community and political leaders to understand the community college mission was one of their greatest challenges. Is that, perhaps, because we are hanging on to the old answers when it is the questions that should be doctrine? What are the educational and training needs associated with today's and tomorrow's societal imperatives and how and where are this education and training to be provided? The answers must be developed anew in light of the changing demographics, technology, and needs of today's citizens. They must be developed in collaboration with those who will be served. As community colleges serve their communities with renewed vigor and vitality, they just might be better understood.

In this book, Vaughan and Weisman have chronicled changes in the characteristics of community college presidents as we have moved from the first to the second or third generation of presidents at most colleges. Most of the founding presidents, and even most of the immediate protégés of the founding presidents, have moved on. The corps of presidents has become more diverse in gender and to a lesser degree in race or ethnicity. Yet one thing has not changed: Presidents need to have a vision of the contributions that community colleges can make to society and the zeal to lead their institutions to accomplish their missions.

DONALD E. PUYEAR

Executive Director
State Board of Directors for
Community Colleges of Arizona

PREFACE

This book provides a snapshot of the community college presidency by studying the personal and professional profiles of community college presidents. The data used in this book come primarily from national studies in which presidents completed a Career and Lifestyle Survey (CLS). In addition, interviews with 13 community college presidents further reveal the challenges that community college presidents currently face and those they will face in the next century.

In 1984, 591 out of 838 public community college presidents (71 percent) participated in the CLS study; in 1991, 837 out of 1,097 public community college presidents (76 percent) participated in the study; and in 1996, 680 out of 926 public community college presidents (73 percent) participated in the study.[1]

The surveys taken in 1984, 1991, and 1996 provide the data for assessing changes that have occurred in the presidency over time. During that 12-year period, some personal characteristics did not seem to change at all, whereas other changes

---

1. See Vaughan, 1986, and Vaughan, Mellander, & Blois, 1994, for a complete description of the results of the first two studies.

are substantial. For example, presidents today come from approximately the same family background as did the presidents in 1984, yet presidents are better educated now than they were 12 years ago. Women and minorities constitute a greater percentage of the presidency today than ever before.

The professional profile of the presidency has changed to some degree. Presidents today are working longer hours and are staying in the presidency longer than they did in 1984. On the other hand, the presidential pipeline has not dramatically changed; the most common position held by presidents before their first presidential appointment is still an administrative position with academic overview.

In 1986, *The Community College Presidency* presented the data collected from the first version of the CLS. Although much has been written about the community college presidency since 1986, this volume is the first work since that time to combine the views of selected presidents with the data from a national survey. We believe that the survey data, in conjunction with the interviews, provide a more comprehensive look at the presidency than could be gained from data or interviews alone.

Chapter 1 presents a backdrop for the 1996 CLS. The characteristics and leadership attributes of the founding presidents are discussed, and the chapter includes comparisons of the founding community college presidency with the current presidency.

A personal profile of current presidents is provided in chapter 2. The demographic characteristics, educational background, family background, and lifestyle background are reported for current presidents and are compared with selected data from the 1984 CLS and the 1991 CLS.

Chapter 3 follows with a professional profile of the presidency. Data regarding the professional background of current community college presidents, their professional activities and perceptions, presidential employment data, and their plans to leave the presidency are revealed. This information is compared with selected data from the 1984 CLS and the 1991 CLS.

In chapter 4, the comments of 13 current community college presidents are shared regarding the community college mission, resources to fulfill the mission, and threats to the community college mission.

Chapter 5 presents an analysis of selected characteristics of the current community college presidents by race and gender. Demographic information, professional characteristics, and presidential perceptions are presented for male Caucasian, female Caucasian, male minority, and female minority presidents. In addition, comments from the presidents interviewed regarding strategies to increase the percentage of female presidents and minority presidents are offered.

In chapter 6, the two major presidential constituencies are discussed: the governing board and the faculty. A case is made that the successful president establishes and maintains close, effective relationships with these two constituencies.

A discussion of the issues that will be faced and the skills that will be needed by future community college presidents is presented in chapter 7. The chapter begins with a synopsis of the responses from the 680 surveys regarding future issues and strategies to respond to the issues. The skills that will be needed by the president of the future are discussed as perceived by the 13 presidents interviewed.

EDITORIAL NOTES

The majority of the statistics in this book were taken directly from the data generated from the three Career and Lifestyle Surveys as opposed to the publications about the studies. When these data are cited, they are referenced by year (1984, 1991, or 1996) only. When data are cited from sources other than the three CLS studies, full citations are provided.

In the 1996 CLS, presidents were given the following categories from which to select when identifying their race or ethnicity: American Indian/Native American, Asian American/ Pacific Islander, African American, Hispanic, White/Caucasian, and Other. (Presidents were asked to select only one category of race or ethnicity.) Throughout the volume, the term *minority* is used for all presidents who selected categories other than White/Caucasian.

Except as indicated in chapter 5, the categories of gender and race or ethnicity are not considered mutually exclusive. In other words, when statistics about women are presented, these numbers include all women, regardless of race or ethnicity. Likewise, when statistics regarding minority presidents are presented, the figures represent both female and male minorities.

The term *president* is used throughout the book, although some individuals may have titles of chancellor, superintendent-president, or director.

METHODOLOGY

The study that lead to the writing of this book was conducted through mail surveys and telephone interviews. Nine hundred twenty-six community college presidents were surveyed by mail (680 responded) and 13 presidents were interviewed.

The populations for this study were the presidents of public community colleges that belong to the American Association of Community Colleges (AACC). At the time of the study, the membership roster for AACC included 1,594 presidents of two-year colleges or campuses. The following factors resulted in the final number of institutions whose presidents were included in the study: Only public community colleges in the United State—including tribal and federal (Indian) community colleges—were studied. Independent or church-related institutions were eliminated. In multicollege districts, where each college earns separate regional accreditation, every college president and the district president were included. In multicampus college districts, where each campus is covered under the regional accreditation of the parent district, campus presidents were excluded and only the college district president was included. Since the study focused on community colleges, branch colleges of universities also were eliminated. Interim or acting presidents were excluded from the study only if they identified themselves as being in an interim position, they had been in their current position for less than one year, and the current interim presidency was their first presidency. The final number of presidents surveyed was 926.

The first survey was mailed mid-May 1996, with a July 8, 1996, cut-off date. A total of 520 (56 percent) valid surveys were received from the first mailing. A second mailing was sent July 13, 1996. The final cut-off date for accepting completed surveys was August 15, 1996. A total of 160 valid responses were received from the second mailing. The final number of valid surveys received and used for this analysis was 680, which represents 73.4 percent of the population. The data include the responses from presidents from 46 states.

Following the analysis of the survey data, in-depth telephone interviews were conducted with 13 presidents: George R. Boggs, Superintendent/President, Palomar College, California; Charles R. Dassance, President, Central Florida Community College; Wayne E. Giles, Chancellor, Kansas City Metropolitan Community College District, Missouri; Zelema M. Harris, President, Parkland College, Illinois; Peter Ku, President, South Seattle Community College, Washington; Gunder A. Myran, President, Washtenaw Community College, Michigan; James R. Perkins, President, Blue Ridge Community College, Virginia; Alex A. Sanchez, President, Albuquerque Technical Community College,

New Mexico; Peter A. Spina, President, Monroe Community College, New York; Linda M. Thor, President, Rio Salado Community College, Arizona; Mary D. Thornley, President, Trident Technical College, South Carolina; Steven R. Wallace, President, Inver Hills Community College, Minnesota; and Desna L. Wallin, President, Forsyth Technical College, North Carolina.

The presidents interviewed represent rural, urban, and suburban colleges from different parts of the country. Male, female, Caucasian, and minority presidents were included. Several of the presidents were in their second presidencies; others had long tenures in their current position. Each of the interviewees was asked the same basic questions with additional questions asked when warranted. The final question gave the interviewees the opportunity to make additional observations on the presidency should they wish to do so. All of the presidents interviewed were asked for and gave their permission to be quoted in this study. Copies of the survey and the interview questions are included as appendixes.

ACKNOWLEDGMENTS

The authors deeply appreciate the cooperation of the 680 presidents who responded to the survey that provided much of the data for this study. A special note of thanks is due to those 13 presidents who agreed to be interviewed for the book. They shared their time, knowledge, wisdom, and experiences freely. Their comments add greatly to our understanding of the presidency.

We have received important support from three members of the Academy for Community College Leadership Advancement, Innovation, and Modeling (ACCLAIM) team. First and foremost, we would like to acknowledge the support we received from Dr. Edgar J. Boone, director of ACCLAIM and William Dallas Herring Distinguished Professor in the Department of Adult and Community College Education at North Carolina State University. Dr. Boone provided the opportunity for both of us to join the faculty at N.C. State and encouraged our scholarship. We have benefited from our affiliation with ACCLAIM and thank Dr. Boone for his generosity and support.

Ruth Shultz, office manager, ACCLAIM, found an answer to

every question we had, knew the proper procedure for every form that needed to be completed, and generally made our entire experience with ACCLAIM a pleasant and memorable one. Ruth is a very kind, caring individual who always makes life easier and more pleasant for those around her. We thank her for her friendship and her assistance.

Carmen Sasser, administrative assistant, gave her eagle eye to many versions of this manuscript. No matter how well we thought we had proofread the materials, Carmen was always able to help us improve the product. She is a pleasure to work with and is always generous with her time and her substantial knowledge.

Robert Pedersen assisted with the development and administration of the survey instrument. Donna Carey, editor of Community College Press, has been very helpful, offering advice and assistance when needed. David Pierce, president of AACC, supported the project from the beginning. His encouragement and support were invaluable. His friendship with the first author has been a source of inspiration for several years.

We appreciate Don Puyear's willingness to do the foreword to the book. His experiences as president of three community colleges and executive director of a state system provide him with a unique perspective on the presidency. The first author has found his friendship and advice invaluable over the years.

The first author wishes to acknowledge the help of Peggy A. Vaughan. As she has done for a number of years, Peggy read the manuscript, making many corrections and offering valuable suggestions.

The second author would like to thank Ken Wayland for his support and for serving as computer guru throughout the project. Kenny was unwavering in his encouragement and willingness to do whatever was necessary to help the second author in the research and writing of this book.

SPECIAL CONTRIBUTOR

The authors wish to thank Sharon D. Buddemeier for the many hours of work she devoted to the study. Sharon, a doctoral student in the Department of Adult and Community College Education at North Carolina State University, spent tireless hours coding, verifying, analyzing, and reanalyzing the data as our understanding of the data increased and our ideas became more focused. We thank Sharon for her support, hard work, and willingness to see the project through to the end. Without her help, the book would be less comprehensive and far behind schedule.

1

◆

BUILDING ON THE FOUNDATIONS

As the nation approaches the new millennium, community
college leaders will surely look back as well as ahead, for
they not only will lead their colleges into a new century but also
will celebrate the 100th anniversary of the founding of Joliet
Junior College (1901), the nation's oldest public junior college.

A major premise of this book is that only with knowledge of
the context in which community college presidents function can
the community college presidency be understood. In addition,
only with some knowledge of the past can the present and
future be understood. Therefore, before moving to the current
status of the community college presidency, this chapter will
look back to the founding presidency of a few decades ago
—the 1960s and the mid-1970s—and present some comparisons with today's presidency.

Many of today's presidents were influenced, mentored, and
trained by founding presidents of the 1960s and 1970s, often
adopting their philosophies and practices. By looking back,
today's presidents can view complex issues and problems
through a historical perspective rather than through the perspective of the latest crisis. And by understanding the role of

the founding presidents, we can appreciate more fully the role of today's community college presidents, who build upon the foundations laid in those earlier decades.

Founding presidents were not that rare in the 1960s and early 1970s, a time during which, in some years, a new community college opened each week. For example, the number of public community colleges increased from 405 in 1960–61 to 1,030 in 1976–77. The period from 1964–65 to 1966–67 saw the opening of 113 colleges (Cohen and Brawer, 1996, p. 15). Each new college president faced a unique situation.

Unfortunately for those who would like to know more about presidential life in the 1960s and early 1970s, much of the intimate history of the boom years of community college development is lost, for it was never recorded. What survives today are facts and figures such as the ones cited above regarding the number of community colleges opening, stories about new states developing community college systems, and "political histories" describing the legislative maneuvering that took place in state after state as legislators jumped on the high-speed community college bandwagon.

Pathways to the Presidency

By 1963–64, the doctorate was becoming the degree of choice for public community college presidents, with almost 58 percent of the 140 new presidents of public institutions appointed to the presidency of public community colleges in that year having a doctorate. Another trend of the mid-1960s was for more community college governing boards to seek presidents from the junior college ranks, with more than 56 percent of the 140 new public community college presidents selected in 1963–64 moving up from within the junior college ranks. The public schools, in turn, were a declining source for presidents, with slightly more than 17 percent of the 140 new public community college presidents coming from that source (almost 31 percent of the public community college presidents came from public schools prior to 1952). Senior colleges and universities provided almost 18 percent of new public community college presidents in 1963–64, with the remaining presidents (8.7 percent) coming from other sources (Schultz, 1965).

Other trends that are evident today in the pathways to the presidency were already taking shape by the mid-1960s. Of the 140 public community college presidents newly appointed in 1963–64, 20 presidents (more than 14 percent) came to the position from another junior college presidency (Schultz, 1965).

By 1970, the percentage of public community college presidents with a doctoral degree had risen to more than 73 percent. More than 18 percent had served as president of another institution before assuming their current position, and more than 42 percent had served as administrators in a public community college before becoming presidents. During a time when moving from one position to another was the norm among community college professionals, the average tenure of community college presidents in their current positions in 1970 was 5.2 years (Burke and Tolle, 1972), indicating a relatively stable presidency.

Some trends going back as far as the 1960s and early 1970s have continued today. The 1996 survey reveals that almost 89 percent of today's presidents have either an Ed.D. or Ph.D. degree. The doctorate is a prerequisite for most presidencies today. Almost 90 percent of today's presidents come from within the community college field, indicating that community college boards tend to choose "one of their own" when selecting a president. The average tenure of today's presidents in their current position is seven and one-half years, giving community colleges greater stability in the leadership at the top. A final trend that can be traced to the 1960s and early 1970s is the trend for presidents to move from one presidency to another. Almost 30 percent of today's presidents have held two or more presidencies in their careers.

Accelerating to the Presidency

In the early 1970s, community colleges were still riding the crest of the boom period of their development, philosophically, financially, demographically, and chronologically. Because of this boom, many people were able to make leaps in their careers that otherwise might not have been possible. A number of universities, with support from the W. K. Kellogg Foundation, developed degrees in higher education with an emphasis on community college education, and a degree from a Kellogg-supported program was valued by those in the position to hire new presidents. The following account by George Vaughan illustrates the rate of advancement that was possible for some aspiring presidents during those years of rapid growth:

> In 1967, I joined Dabney S. Lancaster Community College (DSLCC), a new community college in the new Virginia Community College System, as academic dean. Upon gaining my first taste of administration and 10 months of experience as an administrator, I realized that I knew little about the role of academic dean—or the community college, for that matter—and I wanted to know more. I resigned my position to pursue a degree in higher education.
>
> Upon completing the course work for a Ph.D. in higher education at Florida State University, I joined Virginia Highlands Community College (VHCC), yet another new community college in the Virginia system, as academic dean. After less than two years, I was asked by the chancellor of the Virginia system and by the local college board of a yet-to-be-built community college if I would "consent" to being interviewed for the presidency.
>
> In the summer of 1971, I assumed the presidency of

Mountain Empire Community College, one of the last colleges to join the Virginia system. With a new doctorate, less than three years of administrative experience, an abundance of energy, and little knowledge about the presidency, I took on the task of opening a new community college.

During my interview for the presidency, one board member noted that he knew nothing about selecting a community college president. My response, one that would probably cause me to lose the position today, was that I knew very little about being a community college president. Of the 12 board members, only one had any experience with community colleges, and his experience was limited to less than two years on the board of another new community college. The board and I were probably a good fit, and some would say typical for many community colleges that opened during the years of rapid growth.

The college was located in Big Stone Gap, Virginia. There was no campus, no office, no secretary, no faculty, no students, no curricula, and no buildings. I knew no one in the town or the college's service area who could help me find temporary quarters for the college. I felt as if I were president of nothing.

My first task was to find temporary quarters, my second task to employ a secretary, and my third task to help the secretary clean our temporary quarters. These tasks completed, I set about to employ two deans and a business manager. I made all of the decisions on whom to employ without consulting anyone because there was no one to consult. Making decisions, many of which were precedent setting, came with the territory of being a new community college president.

Founding presidents had to make many decisions, some large and some small, quickly and with little consultation. They often exercised a heavy hand in the early years of a college's operation, thus leading to charges that they were autocrats with little regard for participatory governance or faculty opinions on most subjects. Although some of the charges are justified, it would have been difficult for the founding presidents to have acted differently during the first or second year the college was in operation. Successful presidents moved gradually toward involving more people into the governing process.

Leila Gonzalez Sullivan (1997), president of Essex Community College, Maryland, places the founding presidents in historical context in her article on the evolution of the community college presidency. She notes, "Many of the institutions are making a transition to a third generation of presidents whose leadership style is substantially different from their predecessors—the first generation of 'Founding Fathers,' who pioneered a new and democratic form of higher education, and the second generation of 'good managers,' who led the college through a period of rapid growth and abundant resources" (p. 12). Sullivan also writes:

> The first two generations of presidents had some characteristics in common: they were generally white males, married, in their 50's, who had come up through the academic ranks. They exhibited a traditional leadership style within a hierarchical organizational structure. . . . In many institutions, both the industrial model of collective bargaining and the university model of faculty relations were applied as well. Under these leaders, colleges which started on a shoestring and were creative, daring and unrestricted grew into large bureaucracies with enviable physical plants, vast resources, and considerable community support (p. 12).

The early presidents who were successful were quick studies; they learned a great deal about the community college mission while they were shaping it. Just as important, they learned a great deal about being a president while functioning as one. Presidents read everything they could about the community college. Attendance at the annual meeting of the American Association of Community and Junior Colleges, as it was then called, became mandatory. There presidents met their counterparts, shared experiences, and heard numerous speeches on the community college mission, governance, funding, and other aspects of this rapidly developing phenomenon in American higher education.

Contributions of the Founding Presidents

Perhaps the greatest contribution of the founding presidents was the unbridled missionary zeal they brought to promoting the community college mission, speaking to any group that invited them. The "telling of the story" was an important part of the founding president's role. Although the first public junior college had been in existence since 1901, the idea of a college that proposed to offer something for almost everyone and was within commuting distance of almost everyone was new to the individuals living in thousands of communities across the land. The founding president had to convince members of the community at large that the community college was both legitimate and permanent.

For example, in the early 1970s the anti-poverty programs of the Great Society were in full bloom. These programs came and went, depending upon funding, political support, and accomplishments. Community members, unfamiliar with the community college, often linked it with these short-lived programs, assuming that the community college was just another funded program designed to "enlighten the natives" and probably would not be around for very long. The idea of a college committed to serving its community, while a grand idea, took a lot of convincing before communities bought into this radical departure from higher education as they knew it.

In addition to "selling" the college, the founding president had to build an organization that would support the college's mission, operate efficiently, and establish the college as an integral and legitimate part of higher education. Faculty members, even though they accepted a position at the new community college, often had to be convinced that the community college—their college—was a real college. Over a period of time, largely due to the prominence of the public community college, a new definition of the term *higher education* emerged. The new definition included community colleges as well as four-year institutions.

Many individuals joined the community college faculty with the idea that the position was a stepping-stone to a position in a four-year college, a fallacy in most cases, for many of the faculty recruited in the late 1960s and early 1970s are still teaching in a community college. These early faculty members have provided stability and continuity as community colleges have continued to evolve over the years.

Effective founding presidents brought together faculty, governing boards, staff, students, and community members, creating an important institution that embodied many of the ideas inherent in American democracy. A favorite word of the era, *synergism*, describes best what happened on many campuses as the community college took on dimensions that far exceeded its individual parts.

The founding presidents played a major role in creating the culture of the college they led. Much of the community college's culture formed in the 1960s and 1970s, while always evolving, has endured to this day. Although most of the founding presidents have left the scene, they often have become a part of the college's culture.

Much of the zeal displayed by the early presidents is alive and well today as presidents continue to tell the community college story at Rotary meetings, to the Chamber of Commerce, to PTAs, and, as in the past, to anyone who will listen. Today, many faculty members as well as leaders from business, education, and all segments of society join in the telling of the community college story.

Shortcomings of the Founding Presidents

The major shortcoming of the early presidents was their failure to involve faculty, administrators, support staff, and in some cases the governing board, in governing the college during its first two or three years in operation. It seems that community colleges suffered in at least four areas from the lack of participatory governance:

- The image of the colleges suffered at the hands of much of the rest of higher education. Four-year college faculty and administrators often viewed the community college as adhering too closely to the public school model of governance, with the faculty serving as employees with little input into the operation of the college rather than as colleagues and peers of the president.

- Trustees often took the recommendations of the president as the final word, rarely questioning the president's wisdom, judgment, or fairness. Although the president's voice should be the one trustees hear most often, it is not the only one.

- Faculty members often were intimidated by the president and deans, creating a situation where important voices were ignored. Afraid to speak openly on issues affecting the well-being of the college and therefore their own well-being, faculty members denied the colleges their unique perspective and the knowledge gained from their experiences as faculty members.

- Many presidents who followed the founding presidents continued the practices of their predecessors, extending even in today's colleges some of the negative aspects associated with the above shortcomings. Even in this day, some faculty members are afraid to speak their minds for fear of reprisal from the administration. Fortunately, the majority of today's presidents welcome the faculty and trustees as equal partners in the educational enterprise.

Stress in the Boom Years

Opening a college was stressful. Sometimes almost no one in the area in which the college was located had ever heard of a community college. In essence, the new college had no history, no experience, and no credibility to draw upon. Part of the founding president's role was to bring credibility to an institution that was prepared to open its doors to all comers, including many who were not academically prepared for college-level work. No wonder the members of the community wondered if the community college was going to be a real college.

Making decisions is a source of stress in most organizations. When even minor decisions set precedents that will be followed for a number of years, the stress increases. This was especially true for presidents with little top-level administrative experience.

In addition to worrying about credibility, organizational matters, finances, and decisions, any number of things often went wrong as colleges prepared to open. Furniture did not arrive on time, classrooms were not completed, a faculty member accepted another position at the last moment, and so on.

The greatest producer of stress in the early years may have been enrollments. The question most asked by one president of another during the early years was, "Did you make your enrollment?" To increase enrollment every year became the Holy Grail. To fail to meet one's enrollment projections caused embarrassment and even a sense of failure. Governing boards could not understand why enrollments varied from year to year; presidents had few plausible explanations for the ups and downs of enrollments when a college first opened. Presidents and their teams sought ever new sources of students, often without considering the long-term impact on resources. Many colleges enrolled more students than they were funded for, a practice that would cost community colleges dearly in later years when legislators refused to fund over-enrollments.

An often overlooked issue, and one laden with stress for the true believer in the community college mission of the 1960s and early 1970s, was how the college could fulfill its commitment to open access admissions. That is, how could the college fulfill its mission to admit anyone 18 years of age or older or anyone who was a high school graduate and still maintain academic standards? Moreover, a question asked quite often before the massive student aid programs of the 1970s and later was where members of the lower socioeconomic groups would obtain funds for attending college. These questions haunted presidents who believed that their community colleges must have open admissions, that the people's college must offer something for everyone. A popular cliché of the day was that the community college could and should be all things to all people. The motto itself was enough to produce stress in those presidents who took it seriously.

Tampering with the college's budget is guaranteed to cause stress. Budget freezes and cuts are not new. The early 1970s saw the Nixon freeze on spending and budget cuts from some state capitals. Faculty and administrators did not react favorably to small or zero raises or to staff reductions.

Academic presidents have faced and continue to face any number of issues that produce stress, regardless of the times in which they serve. In referring to the pressures associated with the presidency, Francis Wayland, the highly successful president of Brown (later named Brown University) from 1827 to 1855 and one of the nation's outstanding pre-Civil War college presidents, may have captured for all time the essence of the stress associated with the academic presidency: "I am a perfect drayhorse. I am in harness from morning to night, and from one year to another. I am never turned out for recreation." Upon hearing the school bell opening the school year in 1855 following his retirement, he remarked: "No one can conceive the unspeakable relief and freedom I feel at this moment, to hear the bell ring, and to know, for the first time in nearly twenty-nine years, that it calls me to no duty" (quoted in Crowley, 1994, p. 24).

Today many community college presidents do not take their allocated days of vacation each year. It may be that days away from the office cause presidents to worry more about the college than they do when at work, thus creating more stress than is encountered on the job. Or it is possible that presidents miss the excitement of the position and, in spite of complaints about being overworked, like being "in the harness" more than being "turned out for recreation." It is also possible that some presidents do not want to give the impression that the college can operate effectively for a few weeks without them. In any event, today's presidents are fascinated by the job and continue to serve, some equaling or exceeding Wayland's 28 years in the presidency.

Increased Complexity in the Presidency

In many ways the community college presidency is more complicated today than in the 1960s and 1970s. At some colleges, governing board members have become more intrusive in the management of the college and more political than in the past, often demanding answers that past presidents considered to be none of the board's business. Trustees are also better educated about their duties and know what questions they should be asking, a situation that often was not true in the 1960s and 1970s. Adding to the complications associated with the presidency is that in some cases, would-be trustees base their board election campaign on reining in or throwing out the president. Also, as the nation's population changes, people other than Caucasian men are demanding and gaining representation on the board, thus bringing to the board new perspectives on community needs and the role the community college plays in fulfilling those needs.

The globalization of the economy and the demand for highly trained workers have had an impact on the community college presidency. Most community college leaders in the 1960s and 1970s were concerned with serving only the people within the college's service area and had little regard for global issues such as creating a workforce that would be competitive worldwide. The chancellor of the Virginia Community College System, from the time he assumed the position in 1966 until his retirement in 1979, regularly admonished the presidents in the system to remember that the colleges were created to serve the local population and had no business becoming involved with issues beyond the borders of their service regions and certainly had no reason to be concerned with international education. Today, distance education, the Internet, cable television, and other marvels of modern technology have diminished the significance of service area boundaries. If the local community college cannot fill someone's educational needs, another institution will. Although some semblance of service boundaries may be preserved among public institutions within their own state, out-of-state institutions will not be limited by any such boundary restrictions. So what used to be a rather simple task—defining the college's service area—has become increasingly complex.

Producing graduates who can compete in a world market makes the presidency more complicated today. Partly as a result of the global economy with its demand for highly competent workers, community colleges, and thus community college presidents, are held accountable for how well graduates perform. While accountability is a bandwagon that has made the community college trip many times before, the assessment movement has brought new meaning to accountability within the institution. In addition, companies employing community college graduates want proof that the graduates can perform the jobs for which they are employed. Presidents now know that, up to a point, their effectiveness can be measured by the effectiveness of the college's instructional program. They also know that legislators, employers, and members of the public are asking more questions and demanding more answers regarding how the colleges are preparing a competent workforce. The demand for accountability, while positive for the most part, can make the presidency more complicated than it was in the past.

Presidents in many states no longer base their success on the number of student FTEs generated each year. Nevertheless, enrollments still ultimately drive support for much of higher education. Today, in a matter of seconds, computers generate student demographic data that were impossible for most institutions of higher education to obtain a few years ago. Enrollment projections are much more sophisticated than they were when presidents "prayed a lot" that their colleges would meets their projections.

Yet, as *The Chronicle of Higher Education* (Healy, 1997) reports, projecting enrollments remains far from an exact science. *The Chronicle* observes that the almost universal predicted growth in college enrollment across the nation has not taken place in some states. Indeed, the article notes that "college and state officials say enrollment forecasting has become trickier.

Americans' choices about how and where and when to pursue a higher education are now so varied that current projections in many states need retooling" (p. A23). In Virginia, for example, estimates made in 1995 regarding the number of college students who would enroll in public institutions from 1995 to 2001 were revised in 1997. The result was that the 1997 revisions had estimated that approximately 18,000 fewer students than had been projected in the 1995 study would enroll in the state's public institutions of higher education (p. A24). Even with today's sophisticated methods and tools for projecting enrollments, the president's life is often complicated when it is uncertain how many students will enroll at any given point in time, and as *The Chronicle* points out, the magic formula for projecting enrollments continues to elude educational leaders.

Certainly complicating the presidency today are the changes in funding formulas and sources of funding. Presidents are expected to tap new sources of revenue, including private sources. No longer are most states willing to foot the bill to the extent that they did in the past, especially those states that have passed laws limiting local and state tax revenues. As suggested above, budget cuts are nothing new for community colleges. What is new is that state and local revenues have declined as a percentage of operating costs and are unlikely to reach previous levels in the future. Shortfalls in revenue complicate the presidency, as does the pursuit of new sources of revenue.

The global economy and changes in revenue have encouraged community college presidents to seek new partners from all segments of society, including business and industry, other educational institutions, health care providers, social agencies, and other state, local, and federal agencies and organizations. The list is endless. The president is pulled more and more into the world beyond the campus, devoting more and more time to working with leaders outside the college. Although much good has come from these partnerships, they have not simplified the president's life. As internal and external constituents vie for the president's time, life does become complicated.

Perhaps the major issue complicating the presidency today is the role of technology in higher education. Technology raises issues that were unthinkable only 10 years ago—let alone 30 years ago—including what guidelines are appropriate for defining the college's service area, what instructional methods are best suited to today's world, and what constitutes the role of the faculty member.

Today, most colleges are concerned with communicating their message as widely as possible via technology, even if the majority of their students continue to come from the local area and attend classes on campus. Looking back to the 1970s, some community colleges were prohibited from mailing unsolicited public information material to individuals or businesses outside the college's service area, a form of control that is undesirable and indeed impossible today with the Internet and other forms of technology.

Even though as early as 1970 many colleges struggled with developing new approaches to teaching and learning, including developing and using learning labs and wiring classrooms for television, there was not the pressure then that there is today, with major emphasis on the role of technology in teaching and learning, to integrate computers, videos, and other technologies into every phase of the college's operation. Keeping up with the role and cost of the computer and other technologies certainly complicates the presidency today and probably will do so for years to come.

Further complicating the role of today's president is the need to serve a more diverse population. As the nation's population becomes more diverse, community colleges must respond with programs and courses that reaffirm the community college's commitment to serving all segments of society. Diversity, with its many interpretations and manifestations, must be dealt with effectively; otherwise, community colleges and their presidents will fail to accomplish the college's mission and, therefore, will no longer serve as one of the major avenues through which individuals pursue the American Dream.

Finally, the president-board relationship is changing. No trustee today would dare to suggest that he or she knows nothing about selecting a community college president. The majority of today's trustees are well educated and well informed about their role. The effective president recognizes the important role the board plays and works with it as an equal partner in the educational enterprise.

The community college presidency is more complicated today if for no other reason than American society is more complicated today than in the past. Factors complicating the presidency stem from broad movements within society that are beyond the presidents' control, but presidents must understand and interact with these movements if they are to lead their colleges successfully into the future.

2

◆

A PERSONAL PROFILE
OF THE PRESIDENCY

This chapter focuses on the personal characteristics of community college presidents, their demographic characteristics, their educational background, and their lifestyle choices. The purpose of the chapter is twofold: to present a current profile of community college presidents and to explore changes in the profile between 1984 and 1996. The comparison of the characteristics of the 1984 and the 1996 presidents is based upon data obtained from the Career and Lifestyle Survey (CLS), administered in 1984, 1991, and 1996.[1]

Throughout this book, the profile of the presidents in 1984 is compared to the profile of today's (1996) community college presidents. In cases where the data are not available from 1984, the five-year trend is shown. The majority of the statistics in this chapter were taken directly from the data generated from the three Career and Lifestyle Surveys as opposed to the publications about the studies. When these data are cited, they are

---

1. In various sections of this chapter, the results of the 1991 study are compared to the current study. In order to assure appropriate statistical comparison between the two survey years, the adjusted (relative) frequencies are reported for the 1991 survey data. These figures may differ from the frequencies reported in Vaughan, Mellander, & Blois (1991).

referenced by year (1984, 1991, or 1996) only. When data are cited from sources other than the three CLS studies, full citations are provided.

Except as indicated in chapter 5, the categories of gender and race or ethnicity are not considered mutually exclusive. When statistics about women are presented, these numbers include all women, regardless of race or ethnicity. Likewise, when statistics regarding minority presidents are presented, the figures represent both female and male minorities.

DEMOGRAPHIC INFORMATION

Gender

There was a significant increase in the percentage of female presidents between 1991 and 1996. Of the 679 presidents who responded to the 1996 survey question, nearly 18 percent are female and approximately 82 percent are male. Nearly 11 percent of the presidents were female in 1991.

This finding is among the most important of the 1996 CLS study. The increase in the percentage of women in the presidency can be understood better by looking at those who are hiring the presidents, the literature on the presidency, and those preparing for the presidency. Over the past two decades, awareness of the importance of including women in leadership roles has increased not only within the field of higher education, but throughout all aspects of the United States society. Within the community college ranks, there has been a call by national associations, as well as state boards of trustees, to increase the percentage of women in top leadership positions. These proclamations reflect a commitment by community college presidents and trustees to obtaining diversity within the community college leadership.

The gender breakdown of trustees and presidents reveals that women gained membership on community college boards earlier and in a greater percentage than they did to the presidency. For example, in 1969, during a time of great growth for community colleges and, consequently, a time when new presidents were hired relatively frequently, nearly all of the community college presidents were male, yet 15 percent of the trustees were female (Rauh, 1969).

As time passed, however, the percentage of both female presidents and female trustees increased. In 1987, 29 percent of community college trustees were female (Whitmore, 1987); and in 1995, 33 percent of the trustees were female (Vaughan and Weisman, 1997). By 1996, the percentage of female presidents increased to approximately 18 percent. The increase in female presidents in the 1980s and 1990s may be due, in part, to the relatively high percentage of female trustees during these years.

The literature read by trustees and others who influence the presidential selection process may also affect who is appointed president. Twombly (1995) asserts that the literature on leadership influences the reader's expectations of leaders' style and gender. She found that the majority of writings about community college leadership and the community college presidency has reflected, up to this point, a bias toward characteristics and styles that have been socially construed as attributable to men and not to women. Yet she states that recent research and writings on community college leadership and presidents support "a more gender inclusive interpretation" (p. 75). Twombly's assertion that the literature influences the reader's expectations may mean that those who read current literature about the presidency may change their expectations about community college leaders into more gender-inclusive expectations. In addition, if the writings are based upon the research of current practices, gender-inclusive leadership styles may already exist on community college campuses and in boardrooms.

A look at the presidential pipeline may also shed light on the increase in female community college presidents. As described in more detail in chapter 3, more than one-half (54 percent) of current community college presidents were in positions with chief academic overview before attaining their first presidency. Therefore, a strong source of presidential candidates are positions such as academic deans or vice presidents with academic overview.

How well are women represented in the presidential pipeline? In a 1989 study, women made up approximately 21 percent of the academic deans in community colleges (Vaughan, 1989). Of the female academic deans, 61 percent aspired to the presidency, considering themselves to be in the presidential pipeline.

DiCroce (1995) asserts that among all institutions of higher education, public community colleges are leaders in hiring female presidents. She speculates that two factors contribute to the relatively high percentage of female community college presidents. As institutions that promote open access and inclusiveness, the culture of the community college may be more conducive to having women at the helm than the culture of more elite or selective higher education institutions. Second, DiCroce cites the relative status of community colleges within the hierarchy of higher educational institutions. As the "bottom of the power rung" (p. 80) within higher education, community colleges may be considered to offer the least prestigious presidential appointments within academe. Therefore, she concludes that although women are ascending to the presidency, by becoming presidents of community colleges, women may be viewed as obtaining the least attractive top leadership positions in higher education. Of course, for those individuals who are passionate about the community college mission, community colleges may offer the most desirable presidential position.

Regardless of how or why the percentage of female presidents has increased, the importance of this increase should be recognized. As college presidents, women serve as role models for other women throughout the college community. Female college presidents represent a part of the emerging leadership and may inspire other women to aspire to the presidency. Female college presidents also serve as role models for approximately one-half of all community college students who are women. In addition, community college boards that hire female presidents send an important message about gender inclusiveness throughout the institution and the community.

How female presidents differ from their male counterparts deserves special attention, for the experiences and attributes that women acquire in attaining and maintaining a presidency may be quite different from the experiences of men. Chapter 5 provides an in-depth look at selected characteristics of female presidents and male presidents and the remarks of selected presidents regarding efforts to increase the percentage of women in the presidency.

Race or Ethnicity[2]

Of the presidents who responded to the survey, 85.6 percent are Caucasian and 14.4 percent are minority. By minority group, 5.2 percent of the responding presidents are African American, 4.9 percent are Hispanic, 1.9 percent are Native American, and 1.5 percent are Asian American. Less than 1 percent of the presidents classify themselves in the "other" category in terms of race or ethnicity. (See Figure 2.1.)

---

2. Presidents were given the following categories from which to select when identifying their race or ethnicity: American Indian/Native American, Asian American/Pacific Islander, African American, Hispanic, White/Caucasian, and Other. (Presidents were asked to select only one category of race or ethnicity.) Throughout the volume, the term *minority* is used for all presidents who selected categories other than White/Caucasian.

Figure 2.1   Presidents by Race or Ethnicity

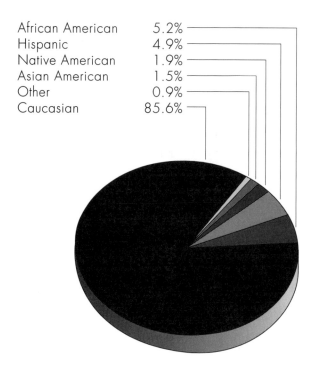

African American	5.2%
Hispanic	4.9%
Native American	1.9%
Asian American	1.5%
Other	0.9%
Caucasian	85.6%

The percentage of all minority presidents increased slightly between 1991 and 1996. Of the 673 respondents to the question on race or ethnicity in 1996, approximately 14 percent are minorities, a 3 percentage point increase from 11 percent of the presidential population in 1991.

Between 1991 and 1996, the rate of increase was greater for some minority groups than for others. For example, African Americans experienced less than a 1 percentage point increase, going from 4.6 percent in 1991 to 5.2 percent in 1996. During the same period, however, Hispanics increased their representation by 2 percentage points, from 2.9 percent to 4.9 percent.

What is known about minorities in the presidential pipeline? A 1989 study in which community college deans of instruction completed the CLS revealed that of the 619 academic deans who responded to the survey, 7 percent were minorities (Vaughan, 1990). In separate surveys for African American and Hispanic academic deans, Vaughan found that few African American academic deans aspired to the presidency, whereas the majority of Hispanic academic deans aspired to the presidents. Yet even if the majority of all minority academic deans aspired to the presidency, the academic dean position is not a plentiful source of prospective minority presidential candidates.

Like female presidents, minority presidents are important to the future of community colleges and their communities. Minority presidents serve as role models for minority students, faculty, other administrators within the community college, and community residents belonging to minority groups. As Eaton (1984) states, "Enlarging the leadership role of women and minorities increases the similarity between the key decision makers and those affected by management decisions" (p. 93). Also, community college boards of trustees can demonstrate a commitment to racial and ethnic diversity through hiring minority presidents.

The fact that minorities have not achieved a substantial increase in the percentage of community college presidencies requires further study. Whereas the factors contributing to the slow increase in minority representation are outside the scope of this study, selected characteristics of the current Caucasian presidents and minority presidents and selected presidents' recommendations for increasing the percentage of minority presidents are explored in greater detail in chapter 5.

Current Age

The average age of all current presidents is 54. The ages of current presidents range from 29 to 72 years old, and the most common age of current presidents (mode) is 58. Fifty-eight percent of current community college presidents are between the ages of 50 and 59, and 93 percent of presidents are between the ages of 45 and 65. (See Figure 2.2 for a breakdown of presidents' ages by ranges.) The average age of presidents has increased since 1984, when the average age of presidents was 51.

The average age of the female presidents who responded to the survey questions is approximately 51 years old and the average age for male presidents who responded to the survey question is 55 years old. The current average age of the minority presidents who responded to the survey question is approximately 53 years old, and the average age for the Caucasian presidents who responded to this question is approximately 54.5 years old.

Figure 2.2 Current Age of Presidents

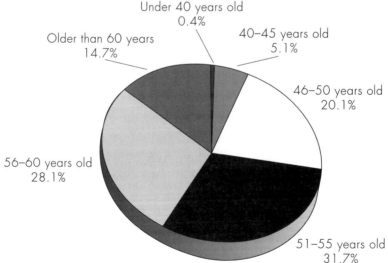

Under 40 years old
0.4%

Older than 60 years
14.7%

40–45 years old
5.1%

46–50 years old
20.1%

56–60 years old
28.1%

51–55 years old
31.7%

Marriage

The marital status of presidents has not changed greatly over the past 12 years. In 1984, 92 percent of the presidents were married and less than 1 percent of the presidents were divorced. Currently, the vast majority of presidents (90 percent) are married. Approximately 65 percent of all presidents are in their first marriage, 20 percent are in their second marriage, approximately 4 percent are in their third marriage, and less than 1 percent are in their fourth marriage. Seven percent of current presidents are divorced and have not remarried, 2 percent are single and have never married, and less than 1 percent are in nonmarried domestic partnerships.

Marital status statistics differ between current male presidents and current female presidents. Approximately 60 percent of all female presidents are married. Forty-two percent of female presidents are in their first marriage, 12 percent are in their second marriage, 4 percent are in their third marriage, 26 percent are divorced, and 9 percent are single and have never married. In contrast, 95 percent of the 556 male presidents who responded to the question on marital status are married, with 70 percent in their first marriage, 22 percent in their second marriage, 3 percent in their third marriage, and 1 president (0.2 percent) is in his fourth marriage. Almost 3 percent of the male presidents are divorced and have not remarried.

A small difference is found between the marital status of Caucasians and minority presidents. Approximately 90 percent of the 575 Caucasian presidents who responded to the question on marital status are married, another 7 percent are divorced and not remarried, and 2 percent are single and have never been married. Similarly, approximately 86 percent of the minority presidents are married, 8 percent are divorced, and 4 percent are single and have never been married.

◆　　　◆　　　◆

The following three demographic questions were added to the 1996 CLS. Presidents were asked to identify their religious affiliation, their political party affiliation, and their political ideology. Since these are new categories for the CLS, no comparison with previous CLS data can be made.

Religion

More than 87 percent of the 659 presidents who responded to the survey question are affiliated with the Christian faith. Sixty-one percent of the presidents are Protestant (21 percent are Methodist, 12 percent are Baptist, 11 percent are Presbyterian, 5 percent are Episcopalian, 4 percent are Lutheran, and 8 percent are affiliated with another Protestant sect). Twenty-one percent of the presidents are Catholic, 2 percent are Jewish, and 10 percent are not affiliated with a religion.

Political Party

The majority of community college presidents are members of the two major political parties. Nearly one-half (47 percent) of the 659 presidents who responded to the survey question are Democrats and 26 percent are Republicans. The remaining 27 percent are independent. (See Figure 2.3.)

Political Ideology

Regardless of political party affiliation, the majority of community college presidents identify themselves as moderates. Approximately two-thirds (67 percent) of the 651 presidents who responded to the survey question consider their political ideology to be moderate, 18 percent consider themselves to be conservative, and 15 percent state that they follow a liberal ideology. (See Figure 2.3.)

Political ideology was analyzed according to political party affiliation. Although the majority of all presidents considered themselves to be moderates, 64 percent of the Democrats, 76 percent of the independents, and 62 percent of the Republicans state that they are moderates. The percentages of presidents who follow liberal and conservative ideologies varied across political party affiliations.

Approximately 27 percent of the 297 Democrats who responded to the survey question stated that they were liberal and approximately 8 percent stated that they were conservative. The proportions were reversed for both independents and Republicans, with a greater difference in percentages between liberals and conservatives among Republicans. Approximately 6 percent of the 173 independents who responded to the survey question stated that they were liberal and approximately 17 percent stated that they were conservative. In contrast, less than 2 percent (3 presidents) of the 168 Republicans who responded to the survey question stated that they were liberal and approximately 36 percent stated that they were conservative.

Figure 2.3 Presidents' Political Party Affiliation
and Political Ideology

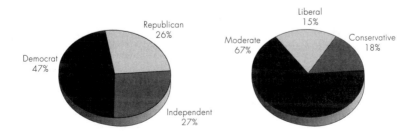

Female presidents are more liberal than are male presidents. Approximately 32 percent of the 114 female presidents who responded to the survey question stated that they were liberal, 61 percent stated they were moderate, and 7 percent considered themselves to be conservative. Of the 536 male presidents who responded to the survey question, 11 percent were liberal, 68 percent considered themselves to be moderate, and 20 percent stated that they were conservative.

Likewise, minority presidents are more liberal than are Caucasian presidents. Approximately 26 percent of the 91 minority presidents who responded to the survey question stated that they were liberal, 64 percent stated they were moderate, and 10 percent considered themselves to be conservative. Of the 556 Caucasian presidents who responded to the survey question, 13 percent were liberal, 67 percent considered themselves moderate, and 19 percent stated that they were conservative.

In what ways do political party affiliation and political ideology affect the community college presidency? Theoretically, although community colleges are public institutions, the community college is considered to be a politically neutral community-based organization. Yet the sociopolitical realities of the community college may override this theory. First, the political ties of community college trustees must be considered, since they are either elected by the public or appointed to their position by an elected official or body.

The debate over whether elected or appointed trustees are better able to maintain a nonpartisan perspective is ongoing. Elected trustees may see themselves as beholden to the party that supported their campaign. On the other hand, appointed trustees may feel obligated to champion the causes of the official who appointed them. In either case, the probability is high that trustees will have strong ties with their political party or with an elected official who has strong ties with a political party. Therefore, the temptation of partisanship exists for trustees and they may or may not yield to this temptation.

Since community college trustees select the president, an important question is how similar trustees' political party and ideological affiliation are to those of presidents. In a 1995 national study of community college trustees, 42 percent of the 599 trustees who responded to the survey question stated that they were affiliated with the Democratic party, 14 percent stated that they were independents, and 43 percent aligned themselves with the Republican party. Moreover, 52 percent of the 603 trustees who responded to the survey question stated that they were moderates, 12 percent considered themselves to be liberal, and 35 percent viewed themselves as conservative (Vaughan & Weisman, 1997). Governing boards, then, appoint presidents who have similar, but not identical, views to the members of the board.

Both political party affiliation and political ideology are relative terms. Whereas one could argue that all Democrats (or all Republicans) are alike, recent political campaigns and national trends point out not only the differences within political parties but the difficulties in clearly differentiating one party from another. Likewise, political ideology is influenced by factors such as geography, culture, or era.

Although the political party affiliation and political ideology of community college presidents may be interesting characteristics to study, the most important point is that these characteristics should not affect the presidency. Regardless of the ties that bind presidents to political parties and ideologies, presidents should be nonpartisan in their actions. The interests and needs that drive presidents' decision making should be those of the students, faculty, administration, and the community at large, not those of political parties. Although it is most likely impossible for presidents to divorce themselves completely from the pressures exerted by political parties and special interest groups, those presidents who are most skilled at keeping these pressures at bay will have more freedom to make decisions free of political influence.

EDUCATIONAL BACKGROUND

Community College Attendance

As in 1991, experience as a community college student is not uncommon for current community college presidents. Forty-one percent of the 673 presidents who responded to the survey question have attended a community college. Of those 274 presidents who have attended a community college, 37 percent earned an associate degree. In other words, 16 percent of all current community college presidents have earned an associate degree. This percentage has not changed since 1991.

Educational Level

Over the past 12 years there has been an increase in the number of presidents who hold a doctorate. In 1996, the vast majority of all presidents (89 percent of the 677 presidents who responded to the survey question) had a doctorate as their highest degree, as compared to 76 percent of presidents in 1984 who held a doctorate. Of the current presidents holding a doctorate, 45 percent hold an Ed.D. and 44 percent hold a Ph.D.

Slightly more than 1 percent of the presidents hold a professional degree as their highest degree. The remaining 9 percent of the presidents who responded to the survey question have a master's degree as their highest degree (8 percent) or hold some other degree (1 percent).

Field of Study

Of the 305 presidents who hold an Ed.D., 71 percent earned it in higher education. In addition, 53 percent of the 296 presidents holding the Ph.D. earned it in the field of higher education. When added together, 62 percent of the presidents who have earned a doctorate hold it in higher education.

Regardless of their level of formal education, for most presidents (57 percent) the major field of study in their highest degree is higher education. This is an increase from 1984, when 47 percent of the presidents had higher education as their major field of study. Four percent of current presidents hold their highest degree in vocational education, 2 percent in adult education, and 9 percent in another field of education. In total, then, 72 percent of current community college presidents have their highest degree in some area of education.

Presidents' major field of study in their master's degree is most likely to be in the behavioral or social sciences (17 percent), higher education (16 percent), or in another field of education (15 percent).

FAMILY BACKGROUND

The occupational and educational characteristics of community college presidents' family background have changed somewhat between 1984 and 1996. In general, however, as was true in 1985, today's community college presidents come from blue-collar backgrounds.

Father's Occupation

According to the 1996 survey results, the most recent full-time occupation of presidents' fathers was skilled worker (24 percent), business owner or manager (14 percent), farmer (13 percent), unskilled worker (10 percent), or sales and service worker (10 percent). Similarly, in 1984, the occupations of the fathers of those presidents who responded to the survey question were primarily as skilled workers in manufacturing, construction, or mechanical repair (24 percent), as administrators or managers (20 percent), and as farmers (16 percent).

Mother's Occupation

The occupations of the 1996 president's mothers were similar to the occupations of the mothers of the 1984 presidents, with the greatest change being that fewer mothers of current presidents work in administrative support and more mothers work in sales and service. The most recent full-time occupation of current presidents' mothers is still most commonly homemaker (55 percent); in 1984, 59 percent of mothers were homemakers.

In 1996, 45 percent of the mothers worked outside the home, with 13 percent working in the field of sales and service, 10 percent in K–12 education, 6 percent in a medical or health-related field, and 4 percent as a business owner or manager. In 1984, 11 percent of those who worked outside the home worked in education, 11 percent worked in administrative support, and 3 percent worked in sales.

Father's Educational Level

The educational level of the fathers of community college presidents has risen since 1984, but only slightly. The majority of the fathers of current presidents (78 percent) have a high school diploma or less. Approximately 44 percent of the presidents' fathers have less than a high school education and 34 percent earned a high school diploma. Similarly, in 1984, 51 percent of presidents' fathers had less than a complete high school education and 29 percent had a high school diploma (for a total of 80 percent with a high school diploma or less). Therefore, the total percentage of presidents' fathers with more than a high school education increased by two percentage points.

In 1984 as well as in 1996, approximately 2 percent of the fathers held an associate degree. A greater number of current presidents' fathers hold a bachelor's degree or higher than did in 1984. Approximately 19 percent of the fathers of current presidents hold a bachelor's degree or higher as compared to 15 percent of the 1984 presidents' fathers who held a college degree.

Mother's Educational Level

The educational levels of presidents' mothers also improved slightly over the past 12 years. In 1996, 30 percent of presidents' mothers held less than a high school diploma compared to 40 percent of the 1984 presidents' mothers who held less than a high school diploma. Approximately 45 percent of the mothers of current presidents earned a high school diploma, whereas 38 percent of the mothers of presidents in 1984 received a high school education. As was found with the presidents' fathers, the total percentage of presidents' mothers who have a high school education or less has not changed greatly since 1984 (78 percent of the presidents' mothers in 1984, as compared to 75 percent of the presidents' mothers in 1996).

Five percent of the mothers of current presidents have earned an associate degree, a percentage that decreased by less than 1 percent since 1984. In 1996, 16 percent of presidents' mothers had earned a bachelor's degree or higher, as compared to 14 percent of mothers who had done so in 1984.

As in the previous study (Vaughan, 1986), today's community college presidents can be viewed as high achievers who, as first-generation college graduates, managed to "leapfrog" to the top of their profession. More than three-quarters of the parents of current presidents did not attend college and the majority worked in occupations that did not require more than a high school education. With close to one-half of the current presidents having attended a community college, the importance of the community college for introducing first-generation college students to higher education is demonstrated in the current presidents' family educational history. The commitment of presidents to the community college mission of access and comprehensiveness may be inspired in part by the presidents' own family background.

THE PRESIDENTIAL SPOUSE

Spouse's Education

The spouses of current community college presidents have attained higher levels of education than the spouses of presidents 12 years ago. Approximately 9 percent of today's presidents' spouses hold a doctorate as their highest degree, 2 percent hold a professional degree as their highest degree, more than one-third (34 percent) of all presidents' spouses have earned a master's degree as their highest degree, 26 percent have earned a bachelor's degree, and 13 percent earned an associate degree as their highest degree. The remaining 12 percent completed a high school education. No spouses of current presidents hold less than a high school diploma.

In contrast, 4 percent of spouses in 1984 held a doctorate , 29 percent held a master's as their highest degree, 34 percent earned a bachelor's as their highest degree, 11 percent held an associate degree as their highest degree, and 2 percent received some other kind of postsecondary diploma or certificate. Eighteen percent of the spouses in 1984 had completed a high school education and 3 percent had less than a high school degree.

Spouse's Employment Status

The employment status of community college spouses has not changed considerably since 1984. In 1984, 36 percent of all spouses were homemakers and 32 percent of the spouses are homemakers today. A majority (68 percent) of the current presidents' spouses work outside the home for pay; 53 percent have a full-time job, and 16 percent work part-time. In 1984, 64 percent of presidents' spouses worked outside the home for pay on either a full-time or part-time basis.

Spouse's Occupation Outside the Home

The most common occupation outside the home among presidents' spouses is still educator. In 1984, 48 percent of those spouses who worked outside the home were employed in some aspect of education. In 1996, of the 403 spouses who were employed outside the home, 43 percent work in the field of education: Approximately 27 percent work in K–12 education, 12 percent work in postsecondary education, and 4 percent work in another area of education.

Age of Spouse

Like the age of the current community college presidents, the average age of presidents' spouses has risen over the past 12 years. The average age of current spouses is 52 years old as compared to an average age of 48 years old for presidents' spouses in 1984.

Similar to the data found regarding the family of origin of community college presidents, today's data on presidents' spouses show they are better educated than they were in 1984, but their employment status and occupations have not changed greatly over the past 12 years.

LIFESTYLE INFORMATION

Geographic Mobility

The percentage of presidents who live in the state in which they graduated from high school has declined over the past 12 years. In 1984, 45 percent of the presidents lived in the state in which they finished high school. In 1996, 39 percent of the 675 presidents who responded to the survey question lived in the state in which they finished high school. Although the percentage of presidents living in the same state in which they finished high school may not have changed dramatically since 1984, it may be of interest to see who out of the current presidents show the greatest geographic mobility.

A greater percentage of male presidents than female presidents live in the state in which they graduated from high school, with 41 percent of the male presidents and 30 percent of the female presidents serving as presidents of colleges in the state in which they graduated high school. The difference between Caucasian presidents and minority presidents is not as great as the difference between men and women; 40 percent of the Caucasian presidents and 36 percent of the minority presidents live in the state in which they finished high school.

Forty percent of the presidents assumed their first presidency in the state in which they finished high school. More than 90 percent of the presidents who assumed their first presidency in the state in which they finished high school currently reside in that state. Of those 245 presidents, 81 percent are in their first presidency, 15 percent are in their second presidency, and approximately 4 percent are in their third, fourth, or fifth presidency. Stated another way, 29 percent of all presidents attained their first presidency in the state in which they graduated from high school and they are still in these positions.

Commuter Marriages

Another measure of geographic mobility, and one that is perhaps more indicative of the national trends, is commuter marriages. Current presidents were asked whether they had commuter marriages and, if they did, who commutes and how far.

Six percent of all married presidents have a commuter marriage. Of the 35 presidents in commuter marriages who responded to the survey question regarding their gender, 34 percent are female and 66 percent are male. Approximately 72 percent of the presidents in commuter marriages are Caucasian and 28 percent are minorities.

Proportionately, a higher percentage of female presidents than male presidents are in commuter marriages and a higher percentage of minorities than Caucasians are in commuter marriages. In other words, 17 percent of the 72 married female presidents and 4 percent of the 535 married male presidents are in commuter marriages. Likewise, 12 percent of the 83 married minority presidents and 5 percent of the 520 married Caucasian presidents have commuter marriages.

The majority of presidents in commuter marriages (61 percent) are in their first presidency; 28 percent are in their second presidency, and 11 percent are in their third presidency.

Presidents who have commuter marriages are themselves the commuter in more than one-half (58 percent) of the marriages. The presidents' spouses commute in 27 percent of the commuter marriages and, in 15 percent of the commuter marriages, both the president and spouse commute.

The most frequent distance traveled by the commuter is up to 100 miles each way. Slightly more than 38 percent of the commuters commute up to 100 miles, 29 percent commute between 101 and 250 miles, 21 percent commute between 250 and 1,000 miles, and 12 percent commute more than 1,000 miles. In addition, 14 percent of the commuters commute daily, 3 percent community twice per week, nearly 52 percent commute weekly, 14 percent commute twice per month, and 17 percent follow another commuting pattern.

The educational level of the spouse in a commuter marriage is higher than that of the majority of spouses. Sixty-four percent of the spouses in a commuter marriage have earned a master's degree or higher. Approximately 28 percent of these spouses have earned a doctoral degree, 6 percent have earned a professional degree, and another 31 percent have earned a master's degree. More than 80 percent of these spouses work outside the home on either a full-time (78 percent) or part-time (3 percent) basis.

The percentage of married presidents who are in commuter marriages is small; therefore, no conclusions about commuter marriages or the individuals in commuter marriages can be made. The fact that presidents are in commuter marriages, however, does raise some important questions. Will more presidents have commuter marriages in the future? If so, what are the implications for the community college presidency, a position that historically has been tied to the community served by the college?

Civic and Social Affiliations

The most popular civic organization to which presidents belong is the Rotary Club; 62 percent of current presidents are members of the Rotary, as were 65 percent of presidents in 1984. Sixty-three percent of Caucasian presidents, 62 percent of female presidents, and 58 percent of minority presidents belong to the Rotary.

The overwhelming preference to membership in the Rotary Club over membership in other civic organizations may be due to the Rotary Club's standing within communities. More than with other civic organizations, Rotary Club membership is valued for making business and community connections. Both membership and service as a Rotary officer have been cited as part of some communities' expectations for community college presidents (Vaughan, 1989).

Community college presidents belong to a variety of other civic, social, and fraternal organizations. Ten percent of all presidents belong to the local Chamber of Commerce, 7 percent are members of the Kiwanis Club, 5 percent belong to the Lions Club, and 4 percent to the Masons. Membership in the Kiwanis, Lions, and Masons by presidents in 1996 is less than it was in 1984, when 12 percent belonged to the Kiwanis Club, 7 percent belonged to the Lions Club, and 10 percent belonged to the Masons.

Four percent of minority presidents and less than 2 percent of female presidents belong to the Kiwanis Club. No female presidents belong to the Lions or the Masons, but 14 percent of female community college presidents belong to the Women's Forum, and 11 percent are members of the League of Women Voters.

Country Club Affiliation

Nearly one-third (31 percent) of the 671 presidents who responded to the survey question belong to a country club. Thirty-four percent of male presidents, 20 percent of female presidents, 34 percent of Caucasian presidents, and 14 percent of minority presidents belong to a country club. Of those belonging to a country club, 79 percent use it for professional entertaining or as a means of carrying out the duties of the position.

Recreation

Presidents participate in sports and other physical activities on a regular basis. Golf remains the most popular sport among community college presidents. Forty-one percent of all presidents play golf on a regular basis, as did 39 percent of the presidents in 1984. Presidents also engage in a number of other sports or activities: fishing (20 percent), jogging (20 percent), tennis (13 percent), swimming (13 percent), walking (12 percent), and skiing (12 percent). In addition, 32 percent stated that they participate in aerobic activities other than those listed on the survey.

Socializing

The majority of presidents find time to relax with friends on a weekly basis. Current presidents were asked whom they see socially at least one hour per week outside of work. (The presidents were asked to circle all that apply, so the total exceeds 100 percent.) Fifty-five percent of current presidents visit socially with colleagues at least one hour per week outside of work, 33 percent socialize with neighbors, 31 percent see church associates socially, and 33 percent visit with club associates. Fourteen percent of the presidents reported seeing no one socially at least one hour per week outside of work.

Presidents reported that their spouses socialize with neighbors (40 percent), professional colleagues (33 percent), church associates (33 percent), and club associates (24 percent) outside of work on a weekly basis. Approximately 8 percent of the presidents reported that their spouses do not socialize with friends at least one hour per week outside of work. Forty presidents (nearly 6 percent) stated that neither they nor their spouse socialize with friends at least one hour per week outside of work.

Annual Leave and Vacation

Current presidents are taking more of their annual leave than they did in the past. Presidents earn an average of 22 days of annual leave each year but use an average of 15 days. In both 1991 and 1984 presidents earned, on the average, 22 days of annual leave, but took an average of 13 days of leave per year. Whatever the reasons are that presidents do not use their annual leave, in most cases, it is not for the purpose of an annual payment of unused time. In 1996, 7 percent of the presidents were paid for unused annual leave at the end of each year.

Approximately one-quarter (24 percent) of all presidents took a vacation that lasted two weeks or more in 1995. Of presidents taking a vacation of two weeks or more, 69 percent performed work related to their duties as president while on vacation, reinforcing the perception that those individuals who occupy the presidency are in the role 365 days per year.

SUMMARY

The percentage of female presidents has increased significantly since 1991, moving from approximately 11 percent of all presidents to approximately 18 percent in 1996. The same percentage increase was not experienced by minority presidents, however. The relatively slight increase from approximately 11 percent in 1991 to approximately 14 percent in 1996 indicates that minority presidents are having less success in increasing their representation in the presidential ranks than are women.

The average age of current presidents is 54 years old. Ninety percent of all presidents are in their first marriage. Presidents tend to be affiliated with the Christian faith, with 61 percent being Protestant and 21 percent being Catholic. Nearly twice as many presidents are Democrats (47 percent) as are Republicans (26 percent). Yet 67 percent of the presidents consider themselves to be moderates.

The educational level of community college presidents rose between 1984 and 1996. In 1984, 76 percent of the presidents had attained a doctorate; in 1996, 89 percent had earned a doctoral degree. Regardless of the level of formal education, more than one-half of the presidents earned their highest degree in the field of higher education.

The community college presidents in 1996 appear to come from a very similar family background to that of the presidents of 1984. In addition, spouses of current presidents have many of the same characteristics that the spouses in 1984 had. The biggest change in the characteristics of spouses of the past 12 years appears to be in the level of education achieved.

3

◆

A PROFESSIONAL PROFILE
OF THE PRESIDENCY

This chapter describes the professional background of current community college presidents, their professional activities and perceptions, presidential employment data, and their plans to leave the presidency. Once again, data from the 1984 CLS are provided when available, thus providing a 12-year perspective on the presidency. If data on a particular topic were not collected in 1984, the data for 1991, when available, are provided.[1] When data are cited from sources other than the three CLS studies, full citations are provided.

The categories of gender and race or ethnicity are not considered mutually exclusive. For example, when statistics about women are presented, these numbers include all women, regardless of race or ethnicity. When statistics regarding minority presidents are presented, the figures represent both female and male minorities.[2]

---

1. In various sections of this chapter, the results of the 1991 study are compared to the current study. In order to ensure appropriate statistical comparison between the two surveys, the adjusted (relative) frequencies are reported for the 1991 survey data. These figures may differ from the frequencies reported in Vaughan, Mellander, & Blois (1991).

2. Presidents were given the following categories from which to select when identifying their race or ethnicity: American Indian/Native American, Asian

PRESIDENTIAL TENURE

The presidents who responded to the survey answered a variety of questions relating to their presidential tenure, such as the total number of years that they have served as community college presidents, the number of years in their current position, and the number of presidencies that they have held. The responses to these and other questions are provided below.

Average Presidential Tenure

Currently, the average total number of years that individuals have spent as community college presidents is 9.8 years. Of the current presidents, one-third have been in the presidency for five years or less. Slightly more than 10 percent of all community college presidents have been in the presidency for one year or less. Twenty-six percent have been presidents from six to 10 years, 18 percent have been presidents from 11 to 15 years, and 22 percent have been in the presidency for 16 or more years. The longest presidential tenure of any community college president is 36 years. (See Figure 3.1.)

Female presidents have approximately half the average presidential tenure of male presidents. The average presidential tenure for female presidents is five years and the average presidential tenure for male presidents is approximately 11 years.

Minority presidents have a shorter average presidential tenure than do Caucasian presidents. The average presidential tenure is almost 7.5 years for minority presidents and Caucasian presidents' average presidential tenure is more than 10 years.

American/Pacific Islander, African American, Hispanic, White/Caucasian, and Other. (Presidents were asked to select only one category of race or ethnicity.) Throughout the volume, the term *minority* is used for all presidents who selected categories other than White/Caucasian.

Figure 3.1   Presidential Tenure

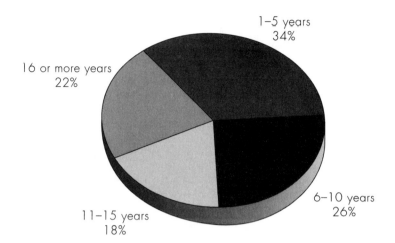

Number of Years in Current Position

The average number of years that presidents have spent in their present position is 7.5 years. This figure has remained relatively constant for the past 12 years; the average in 1984 was 7.3 years.

In 1984, slightly more than one-half (51 percent) of all presidents had been in their current position for five years or less, 22 percent had been in their position for six to 10 years, and 27 percent had been in their position for 11 or more years. In 1996, nearly one-half of all current presidents (47 percent) have been in their present position for five years or less (16 percent of all presidents had been in their current position for one year or less). Another 27 percent have been in their current position for six to 10 years, and the remaining 26 percent have been in their current position for 11 or more years. (See Figure 3.2.)

Figure 3.2   Years in Current Position

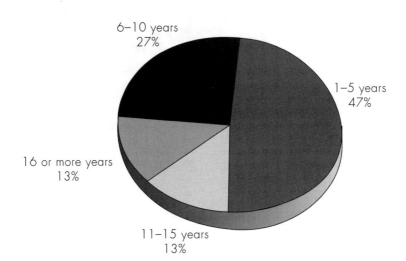

A few of the current presidents may be the founding president of their community college, since seven presidents (less
than 1 percent of all presidents) have been in their current position since the 1960s. The longest time that any of the current
presidents has spent in one position is 31 years.

Number of Presidencies

The majority of current presidents have held only one community college presidency, although the percentage of presidents holding more than one presidency has increased since
1984. Approximately 70 percent of current presidents have
held one community college presidency; nearly 21 percent of
the presidents are in their second presidency; slightly more
than 6 percent are in their third presidency; more than 2 percent

are in their fourth presidency; and less than 1 percent are in their fifth presidency. (See Figure 3.3.) In 1984, 75 percent of the presidents held one presidency; 19 percent were in their second presidency, 5 percent were in their third presidency, 1 percent were in their fourth presidency, and less than 1 percent were in their sixth presidency.

The majority of female presidents are in their first presidency. Of the 119 female presidents who provided the number of presidencies that they had held, 80 percent are in their first presidency; 19 percent are in their second presidency; and 2 percent are in their third presidency.

Of the 94 minority presidents who responded to the survey question, 59 percent are in their first presidency, 27 percent are in their second presidency, 9 percent are in their third, 5 percent are in their fourth, and 1 percent has had five presidencies.

In comparing data for all presidents from 1991 and 1996, the average years in the current position hardly varied (7.26

Figure 3.3   Total Number of Presidencies

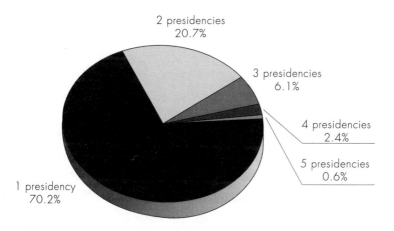

percent in 1991 and 7.52 percent in 1996) and the percentage of presidents with one presidency has not changed substantially, indicating that in general, presidential mobility has not changed much over the past five years. Therefore, the facts that minorities have approximately one-half the average number of years in their current position and have a greater percentage of presidents in more than one presidency than do Caucasians indicate that minority presidents have different presidential employment patterns than do Caucasian presidents. Whether the differences are positive or negative is outside the scope of this study. However, the results of the 1996 CLS indicate that women have been more successful in attaining presidencies than have minorities, but minority presidents have been more successful in moving into subsequent presidencies than have female presidents.

MOVING INTO THE PRESIDENCY

Specific data on attaining the presidency were gathered with the CLS. Presidents were asked at what age they attained their first presidency, which position they held prior to attaining their first presidency, and whether they moved into their current position from another community college presidency.

Age at First Presidency

Six hundred seventy-one presidents responded to the question regarding their age upon assuming their first presidency. Of these presidents, 25 percent attained their first presidency when they were between the ages of 26 and 39 (two-thirds of these were 35 or older); approximately 53 percent attained their first presidency when they were in their 40s; approximately 21 percent attained their first presidency when they were in their 50s; and less than 1 percent were 60 or older when they were first hired into the presidency.

The average age at which all presidents assumed their first presidency has increased slightly, from age 43 in 1991 to age 44 in 1996. This relatively small increase reflects a shift from younger first-time presidents hired before 1991 to relatively older first-time presidents hired after 1991. Whereas the most common age range for attaining a first presidency is still between 40 and 50, in 1996 a smaller percentage of presidents than in 1991 assumed their first presidency before the age of 40 and a greater percentage of presidents were in their 50s at the time of their first presidency. Women assumed their first presidency at a later age than did men; and minorities assumed their first presidency at a later age than did Caucasians.

A comparison of the presidents who have been in the presidency 11 years or more with those in the presidency for 10 years or less revealed that boards are hiring older first-time presidents.

Position Held Before First Presidency

Academic administration still provides the most common route to the presidency. The position that the majority of presidents held prior to their first presidency was chief academic officer (40 percent) or vice president with an academic overview (14 percent). In other words, 54 percent of the current presidents were in positions with academic overview before attaining their first presidency.

This branch of the traditional career pathway has remained constant over the past 12 years. In 1984, the position most frequently held prior to attaining the first presidency was the dean of instruction position, with 38 percent of all presidents coming from this position. Another 12 percent of the presidents in 1984 came from the position of vice president, although it is not known if the vice presidency included an academic overview.

The remaining 46 percent of the 1996 presidents entered their first presidency from a variety of positions. The position held by the second highest percentage of presidents was chief student affairs officer, with 7 percent holding this position before their first presidency. In descending order after these two positions, 5 percent of the presidents held vice presidencies without academic overview, 3 percent were chief business officers, and 3 percent were in continuing education. As addressed in chapter 5, these percentages indicate that those who aspire to a presidency can increase their chances by being in the academic pipeline. (See Figure 3.4.)

Internal Candidacy

One-third of current presidents (33 percent) were internal candidates at the college at which they assumed their first presidency. This percentage is the same regardless of gender or race or ethnicity.

Internal candidates are more likely to have held the positions of either chief academic officer or vice president with academic overview than are candidates selected from outside the institution. Approximately 54 percent of the internal candidates and 49 percent of the external candidates were chief academic officers or vice presidents with academic overview before attaining their first presidency.

Moving into a Second Presidency

Approximately 27 percent of the current community college presidents were serving as presidents at another community

Figure 3.4   Position Held Before First Presidency

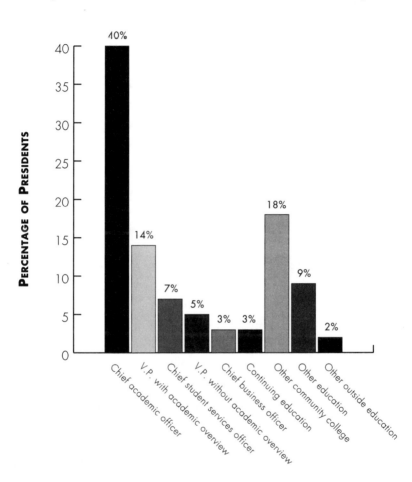

college when they were appointed to their current position. Of these 183 presidents, 67 percent are in their second presidency, 22 percent are in their third presidency, and 11 percent are in their fourth or fifth presidency.

The data suggest that presidents not only move from presidency to presidency, but some move in and out of the presidency. Approximately 30 percent of the current presidents have held two or more presidencies. Of the 200 individuals holding more than one presidency, 86 percent moved into their current position from another community college presidency. Conversely, 14 percent of the current presidents who have held two or more presidencies did not come from a presidential position. Data are not available on the position these presidents held before their current position.

PROFESSIONAL ACTIVITIES

Time on the Job

Current presidents estimated that they spend an average of 57 hours each week performing the duties associated with the president's office, an increase of two hours from the average time they spent working in 1991. A majority of the current presidents (71 percent of the 662 presidents who responded to the survey question) stated that they worked more than 50 hours per week. In contrast, in 1984, 56 percent of the presidents stated that they worked more than 50 hours per week.

Developing a clear picture of the actual amount of time that presidents spend per week is difficult. The duties of the presidency vary. During times of crisis, the president may be called upon to spend up to 18 hours per day, seven days per week, on college matters. In times of stability, the demands are much less. Likewise, bond campaigns, contract negotiations, or other special or seasonal activities require additional presidential time and effort.

No president has the time or inclination to keep a daily log of hours spent working; therefore, the question "How many hours each week do you spend performing the duties associated with the president's office?" really asks, "How many hours does it feel like you work each week?" How one responds to this question may depend on one's feelings of stress, exhilaration, or fatigue at the time the individual responds to the question.

Finally, each president defines the duties associated with the president's office differently. Some may say that since the president cannot escape the presidential role whenever she or he is active in the community, the president is always performing duties associated with the office. Others may feel that activities such as belonging to the Rotary Club or the United Way are personal choices and, therefore, are not part of presidential duties.

Although the specific numbers are inexact, with 91.5 percent of the presidents stating that they work 50 or more hours per week, there is no doubt that the presidency is a time-consuming profession. Moreover, as stated in chapter 2, 69 percent of the presidents who had taken a vacation of at least two weeks in 1996 reported that they had performed work related to their duties as president while on vacation.

Community College Teaching Experience

A background in teaching is a common characteristic for community college presidents, with the vast majority (85 percent) of all presidents having experience teaching at a community college. Forty-four percent of current presidents have taught full-time and an additional 41 percent have taught part-time at a community college. Fourteen percent of all presidents currently teach at their community college at least once a year.

Professional Organizations

Presidential membership in professional organizations has declined over the past 12 years. Although more presidents held membership in the American Association for Higher Education

(AAHE) than in any other organization in both 1984 and 1996, even AAHE is experiencing a decline in community college presidential membership. Approximately 31 percent of all current presidents are members, a substantial decrease from 1984 when 53 percent of all presidents were members.

Approximately one-fourth (24 percent) of current presidents are members of the education honorary fraternity Phi Delta Kappa (PDK), as compared with the 62 percent who were members of PDK in 1984. Almost 14 percent of the presidents in 1996 were members of the National Association of College and University Business Officers (an institutional membership), a decrease from 25 percent of presidents who were members in 1984. All of the presidents surveyed are members of AACC. Membership in professional organizations other than AACC is shown in Figure 3.5.

With the emphasis on building community partnerships and coalitions, membership in Rotary and other civic organizations may seem sufficient for many presidents, thus lessening the perceived need to join professional organizations.

Publishing

Community college presidents contribute to the knowledge in their field through writing and publication. In all three CLS studies, a number of presidents reported having their works published. In 1996, presidents were asked to list all items published while in the presidency. The data from the two previous studies are included in the discussion, although they were collected using time-limited questions and the responses are not directly comparable.

In 1984, presidents were asked to identify their most recent publication. The greatest percentage of presidents had written articles. Of the 504 presidents who responded to the question,

Figure 3.5   Presidential Membership in
Professional Organizations

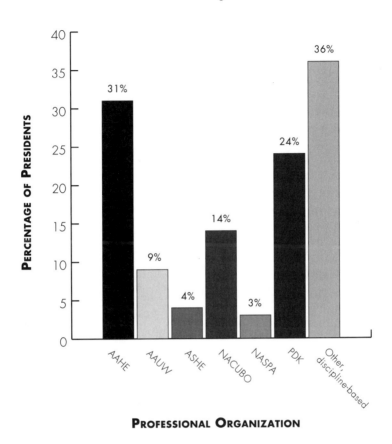

Note: Presidents were asked to check all professional organizations to which they belong; therefore, the total percentage exceeds 100 percent. All of the presidents surveyed are members of AACC.

73 percent had most recently had an article published. (The type of publication, whether newspaper or professional journal, is unknown.) The other types of writing they had most recently published were book chapters (8 percent), books (7 percent), book reviews (3 percent), and other publications not specified on the CLS (19 percent).

In 1991, the survey question was broadened to include publications in the preceding five years. Of the 837 survey participants, 37 percent had an article published in a professional or trade journal; 3 percent had written a chapter in a book; 2 percent had a book or monograph published; and less than 1 percent had a book review published in a professional or trade journal.

In 1996, presidents were asked to identify all publications that they had written while in the presidency. Approximately one-half of all current presidents have submitted one or more manuscripts for publication while they were president and have had at least one manuscript published. Presidents tend to write articles, as opposed to books or book chapters. More than 35 percent of all presidents have had an article published in a professional or trade journal and nearly 35 percent of all presidents have had an opinion article published in a newspaper.

In addition, almost 20 percent of all presidents have written a chapter in a book; approximately 10 percent of all presidents have had a book or monograph published; and nearly 9 percent of all presidents have had a book review for a professional or trade journal published while president. Another 10 percent of all presidents have had another type of writing published. Figure 3.6 shows the kinds of manuscripts that presidents have had published.

In 1986, community college presidents ranked publications as the least important skill or ability for the presidency (Vaughan, 1986, p. 188). Yet the results of the three CLS studies indicate that a strong percentage of presidents are publishing and that the percentage may be increasing. Although community college presidents may not suffer from the publish-or-perish expectation, presidents apparently sense the power of the written word and believe that part of their responsibility as leaders is to share their knowledge and experience with others through writing.

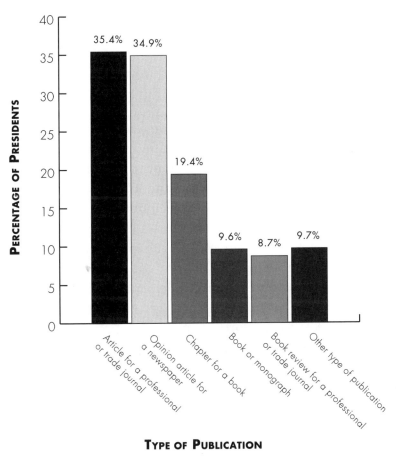

Figure 3.6   Publications by Presidents

Note: Since the presidents were asked to identify all their publications, the total percentage exceeds 100 percent.

PRESIDENTS' CONFIDANTS

Presidents were asked to identify their chief confidant on campus and off campus. In 1996, the presidents most frequently stated that their chief confidant on campus was in one of three positions: chief academic officer (selected by 28 percent of the presidents), another vice president (selected by 24 percent of the presidents), or chief business officer (selected by 21 percent of the presidents). Four percent of all presidents stated that they confided in no one on their campus.

The same three positions were ranked highest in 1984. One-quarter of the presidents identified the chief academic officer as the chief confidant; 13 percent identified the business officer as the chief confidant, and 11 percent identified another vice president as the chief confidant on campus. Although in 1984 none of the presidents stated that they confided in no one, 10 percent of the presidents in 1984 responded with "it depends."

The persistence of the chief academic officer as being the position identified most frequently as the president's chief confidant reinforces the importance of the chief academic officer position. As will be discussed in chapter 6, the two most important presidential constituencies are the board and the faculty. It is most likely no coincidence that the person responsible for working most closely with the faculty is considered an appropriate confidant. Furthermore, presidents may feel a kinship with the person in the chief academic officer position, for the majority of them share similar experiences and backgrounds.

In 1996, the CLS was expanded to ask presidents to identify their chief confidant off campus. The presidents' chief confidant off campus was most frequently either their spouse or partner (31 percent) or another community college president (29 percent). Approximately 10 percent of the presidents confide primarily in the board chair and 5 percent confide in their friends.

The 1991 CLS did not ask presidents to differentiate between on-campus and off-campus confidants. Although the percentages cannot be compared because the questions on the 1991 and 1996 surveys were asked and answered differently, of the off-campus confidants identified in 1991, the two positions mentioned most frequently were the same as the ones identified in 1996. In 1991, nearly 26 percent of the presidents stated that their chief confidant was their spouse, and another 17 percent stated that their chief confidant was another community college president.

PERCEPTIONS ABOUT THE POSITION

In 1991, two questions were added to the CLS: "Do you consider the community college presidency to be a high-risk, moderate-risk, or low-risk position?" and "Do you consider the community college presidency to be a high-stress, moderate-stress, or low-stress position?" The responses of current presidents are compared with those received in 1991.

Perceptions of Risk

Current presidents perceived the level of risk associated with the president's office at a level similar to the level perceived in 1991. In 1996, 40 percent of all presidents considered the presidency to be a high-risk position and 54 percent of the presidents believed the presidency to be a moderate-risk position. In 1991, 39 percent of the presidents determined the presidency to be high risk and 55 percent considered the position to have a moderate level of risk.

In 1991, 39 percent of the responding male presidents and 43 percent of the responding female presidents considered the presidency to be a high-risk position. The situation has not radically changed in the past five years, although a smaller percentage of men and a larger percentage of women considered the presidency to be a high-risk occupation. In 1996, 38 percent of the 551 male presidents responding to this question ranked the presidency as high risk, and 49 percent of the 120 responding female presidents ranked their position as high risk.

The results appear to be more stable when comparing Caucasian presidents and minority presidents, even though the percentage of minority presidents who perceived the presidency as high risk increased slightly between 1991 and 1996. In 1991, 38 percent of the Caucasian respondents and 50 percent of the minority respondents stated that the presidency was a high-risk position. In the current study, 38 percent of the 569 Caucasian presidents and 53 percent of the 96 minority presidents who responded to the question ranked the presidency as high risk.

The perception of the presidency as a position of high or moderate risk seems to diminish with a president's age. Forty-six percent of the current presidents less than 50 years old, 40 percent of the presidents in their 50s, and 34 percent of the presidents 60 years or older perceived the presidency to be a high risk position. Conversely, 49 percent of the presidents less than 50 years old, 53 percent of the presidents 50 to 59 years old, and 63 percent of the presidents who are 60 years of age or older perceive the presidency to be of moderate risk.

Perceptions of Stress

The current presidents' perception of the level of stress associated with the presidency was also similar to the views of their 1991 counterparts. Fifty-two percent of all presidents in 1996 considered the presidency to be a high-stress position, as did 53 percent of presidents in 1991. Forty-seven percent of current presidents considered the presidency to be moderately stressful, as did 44 percent of the 1991 presidents.

Fifty percent of the 551 male presidents responding to this question ranked the presidency as high stress, and 62 percent of the 118 responding female presidents ranked their position as highly stressful. These responses are similar to those found five years earlier. In 1991, 51 percent of the male presidents and 67 percent of the female presidents viewed the presidency as a high-stress position.

A larger percentage of minority presidents than Caucasian presidents felt that the presidency was a high-stress position, but the difference between the two groups is not as great as that between male and female presidents. Approximately 52 percent of the 569 Caucasian presidents and approximately 56 percent of the 95 minority presidents ranked the presidency as a high-stress occupation. In 1991, more than 52 percent of the Caucasian presidents and 61 percent of the minority presidents felt that the presidency was a high-stress position.

The gap between the perceived stress levels of minority and Caucasian presidents appears to be closing, as does the gap between female and male presidents. However, the data reveal that more minority presidents than Caucasian presidents and more female than male presidents still perceive the position to be one of high stress.

As with risk, the perception of the presidency as a position involving high or moderate stress appears to diminish with age. Nearly 60 percent of the current presidents who are younger than 50 years old, 51 percent of the presidents who are between the ages of 50 and 59, and 47 percent of the presidents who are 60 years of age or older perceive the presidency to be a high-stress position. Conversely, 39 percent of the presidents less than 50 years old, 47 percent of the presidents in their fifties, and 51 percent of the presidents who are 60 years old or older perceive the presidency to be a position of moderate stress.

Perceptions of risk and stress are subjective. Stress and risk may be considered positive, motivating factors by some presidents and negative, even debilitating, factors by other presidents. Regardless of whether the interpretations by presidents of the risk and stress levels of the presidency are positive or negative, presidents are clearly stating that at least some risk and some stress are associated with the presidency.

Learning to deal with stress is an important aspect of effective leadership, and the 1996 data indicate that at least some presidents have ways to cope with this stress. For example, one strategy that presidents may use for dealing with the stress of the position is participating regularly in sporting or physical activities. One veteran president interviewed in 1986 (Vaughan, p. 132) suggested that research and writing are effective stress-management tools. Current presidents may agree, since, as indicated earlier, at least one-third of current presidents have had one or more of their works published. Presidents also find time to socialize for one hour or more per week outside of work, although less than one-quarter (24 percent) of all presidents take a vacation of at least two weeks each year.

EMPLOYMENT INFORMATION

The 1996 CLS asked presidents to provide information regarding the conditions of their employment, including the type and length of their employment contract, and housing benefits. All three surveys asked presidents how many days of annual leave they earn.

Employment Contract

Presidents typically have either a rolling (44 percent) or a fixed (39 percent) contract. Sixteen percent of presidents serve at the will of the board.

Those presidents who have employment contracts were asked the number of years the contracts cover. The length of most presidential employment contracts is between one and four years. Eighteen percent of the presidents with employment contracts have one-year contracts, 27 percent have two-year contracts, 24 percent have three-year contracts, and 31 percent have contracts for four years.

Housing

A small percentage of community college presidents receive either housing or a housing allowance as part of their employment agreement. Nine percent of the current community college presidents live in a college-owned house, a slight decline from 1991 when 10 percent of presidents lived in a college-owned house. A slightly higher percentage of the current presidents not living in a college-owned house receive a housing allowance than did their counterparts five years ago. Seventeen percent of the 620 presidents not living in college-owned housing receive a housing allowance, as compared to 16 percent of the 752 presidents in 1991 who did not live in college-owned housing and received compensation for housing. Of the 105 presidents receiving a housing allowance in 1996, 63 percent receive less than $1,000 each month and 37 percent receive $1,000 or more monthly.

Annual Leave

In 1996, presidents earned an average of 22 days of annual leave each year, essentially the same as they earned in 1984. For the great majority of presidents, unused annual leave does not transfer into cash compensation. In 1996, 7 percent of the presidents were paid for unused annual leave at the end of each year.

LEAVING THE PRESIDENCY

Moving to Another Position

Current presidents' plans for leaving the presidency for another position are very similar to those in 1984. Approximately one-fifth (21 percent) of current presidents are very likely to seek another full-time position within the next five years, the exact percentage of presidents in 1984 who felt that it was very likely that they would move to another position within the subsequent five years. Furthermore, another 24 percent of the 1996 presidents stated that it was somewhat likely they would seek or accept another position within the next five years; 29 percent of the presidents in 1984 stated that it was somewhat likely they would do so.

In 1984, it was found that those presidents who had been in their current position for 10 years or less were more likely to move within the subsequent five years than those who had been in their position for more than 10 years. Similar results were found in 1996. Slightly more than one-half (51 percent) of the presidents who had been in their current position for 10 years or less felt that it was very likely or somewhat likely that they would seek or accept another position within the next five years. On the contrary, of the presidents who had been in their position for more than 10 years, approximately one-quarter (28 percent) stated that it was likely they would do so.

Male presidents appear less likely than female presidents to move from their present positions, with 19 percent stating that it was very likely and 23 percent stating that it was somewhat likely that they would seek or accept another position. Female presidents, on the other hand, were more interested in moving out of their current positions, with 33 percent stating that it was very likely and 25 percent stating that it was somewhat likely they would seek another position within the next five years.

Minority presidents were more interested than Caucasian presidents in moving to another position within the next five years. Thirty-three percent of the minority presidents indicated that it was very likely and another 22 percent stated that it was somewhat likely that they would seek or accept another position within the next five years. Approximately 20 percent of the Caucasian presidents stated that it was very likely and another 24 percent stated that it was somewhat likely they would seek or accept a new position within the next five years.

The Next Position. Those presidents who stated that they were very likely or somewhat likely to seek or accept another position in the next five years were asked to what position they would move. The data reveal that presidents plan to stay in education, primarily at the postsecondary level. The overwhelming majority of current presidents who would consider moving to a new position within the next five years plan to move into another community college presidency. Of the 303 presidents who stated that they were very likely or somewhat likely to move within the next five years, 73 percent plan to move into another community college presidency within the next five years. Looking at these numbers another way, 32 percent of all current presidents plan to move into a new presidency within the next five years.

Another 6 percent of the 303 presidents who are very likely or somewhat likely to move to another position within the next five years plan to move into the position of president or chancellor of a state community college system, 5 percent plan to move into the university professoriate, and 4 percent plan to move into a four-year college presidency. Less than 7 percent of the respondents stated that they would move into a political or governmental position or into the private sector.

Approximately 81 percent of the 68 female presidents who were likely to seek or accept another position stated that they plan to move into another community college presidency and another 3 percent planned on becoming the chancellor of a state community college system. Approximately 70 percent of the 235 male presidents who were likely to seek or accept another position within the next five years planned to move into another community college presidency, and another 6 percent planned to move into a state system chancellorship.

Of the 51 minority presidents who were likely to seek another position, 63 percent were also interested in moving into another community college presidency and 10 percent planned on seeking the position of state system chancellor. Approximately 75 percent of the 249 Caucasian presidents who were likely to seek another position within the next five years planned on moving into another community college presidency and more than 4 percent of the Caucasian presidents planned on becoming a state community college system chancellor.

Retirement

An alternative to leaving one's current position by moving to another position is to retire. Almost one-half (45 percent) of the 666 community college presidents who responded to the survey question plan to retire from the presidency within the next six years. Nearly 18 percent stated that they plan to retire from the presidency within the next three years, and 27 percent plan to retire within the next four to six years. Another 23 percent plan to retire within the next seven to 10 years, and the remaining 32 percent plan to remain in their presidency for at least another 10 years. (See Figure 3.7.) Male presidents are more likely to retire in the next six years than are female presidents. Caucasian presidents are more likely than minority presidents to retire in the next six years.

Figure 3.7 Presidents' Plans to Retire

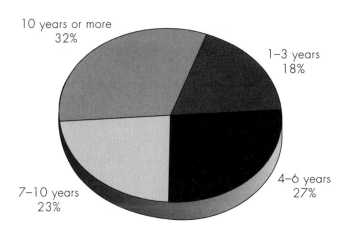

The average age in which all presidents plan to retire is 63 years old, regardless of whether they plan to retire in three, five, or 10 years. Some presidents seem to be preparing for approximately 15 to 18 years in the presidency, since the average tenure of those presidents planning to retire in the next three years is 15 years in the presidency; the average tenure of those presidents planning to retire within the next four to six years is 12 years in the presidency, and the average presidential tenure of those presidents planning to retire within the next seven to 10 years is eight years in the presidency.

As would be expected, those presidents who have been in the presidency the longest are planning on retiring the soonest. Of the presidents with an overall presidential tenure of 16 years or more, 74 percent plan to retire within the next six years; 45 percent of the presidents with a tenure of six to 10 years are

planning to retire within the next six years; and 20 percent of
the presidents with a tenure of one to five years are planning to
retire within the next six years.

A large percentage of vacancies in presidential positions
may occur within the next five to six years. Approximately 45
percent of the current presidents stated that they are very likely
or somewhat likely to seek or accept another position within
the next five years. In addition, the same percentage of current
presidents stated that they plan to retire within the next six
years. Calculating for nonduplication, 79 percent of the 660
presidents who responded to both the survey question about
seeking another position and the survey question about when
they plan to retire stated that they were very likely or somewhat likely to seek or accept another position within the next
five years or that they were planning on retiring within the
next six years.

SUMMARY

Current presidents are remaining in the presidency longer than
they did in 1984, and a greater percentage of current presidents
hold more than one presidency than was the case in 1984.
Current presidents were slightly older than were presidents in
1991 when they obtained their first presidency. The position
with academic overview, such as chief academic officer or academic vice president, remains the most frequently held position
prior to attaining a presidency, with 54 percent of all presidents
coming into the presidency from these two positions. One-third
of the presidents were internal candidates at the college at
which they assumed their first presidency.

Current presidents are spending long hours performing
duties associated with the president's office, with more than 91
percent stating that they work 50 or more hours per week.

Some presidents include in their duties teaching responsibilities; 14 percent of all presidents currently teach at their community college at least once per year. In addition, one-third of all current presidents have contributed to the literature by writing opinion articles for newspapers, articles for professional or trade journals, chapters in books, books or monographs, and book reviews. Almost one-half of the presidents stated that they plan to retire within the next six years.

4

---◆---

MISSION AND MILIEU:
VIEWS FROM THE TRENCHES

To add perspective to the survey results, telephone interviews were conducted with 13 community college presidents in order to present the views of those who have the major responsibility for leading the nation's community colleges. The presidents represent rural, urban, and suburban colleges from different parts of the country; men, women, Caucasians, and minorities are represented. Several are in their second presidencies; others have long tenures in their current position. Each of the individuals interviewed was asked the same basic questions with additional questions asked when warranted. The interviewees also were given with the opportunity to make additional observations on the presidency. After hearing the purpose of the interview and granting permission to be recorded and quoted, each president was asked a series of questions. In this chapter and subsequent chapters in which interview responses are presented, interview questions are indicated by the letter Q. (See appendix B for the complete list of interview questions.)

The following presidents were interviewed:

- George R. Boggs, Palomar College, California
- Charles R. Dassance, Central Florida Community College
- Wayne E. Giles, Kansas City Metropolitan Community College District, Missouri
- Zelema M. Harris, Parkland College, Illinois
- Peter Ku, South Seattle Community College, Washington
- Gunder A. Myran, Washtenaw Community College, Michigan
- James R. Perkins, Blue Ridge Community College, Virginia
- Alex A. Sanchez, Albuquerque Technical Community College, New Mexico
- Peter A. Spina, Monroe Community College, New York
- Linda M. Thor, Rio Salado Community College, Arizona
- Mary D. Thornley, Trident Technical College, South Carolina
- Steven R. Wallace, Inver Hills Community College, Minnesota
- Desna L. Wallin, Forsyth Technical College, North Carolina

FULFILLING THE MISSION

Q: On the survey, presidents were asked to identify the most critical issue facing the community college in the next few years. At the top of the list was a lack of resources required to accomplish the college's mission. Do you agree that your community college does not have adequate resources to fulfill its mission?

> If yes, how has the college's mission been altered as a result of inadequate resources? What steps have you taken to obtain additional resources? If no, what have you done as president to assure that your college has adequate resources to fulfill its mission?

Some, but not all, of the presidents were quick to agree that yes, their college's mission has been altered due to a lack of adequate resources. Others of those interviewed hedged on their answers, noting that factors other than resources had come into play that influence the mission. Others stated that a lack of resources had done little to alter the college's mission. The responses varied not so much because of adequate or inadequate resources but rather because of the ways the presidents defined the mission of their institutions in relation to the resources available. That is, two colleges may have essentially the same resources, yet one president might answer that the resources are inadequate to fulfill the college's mission, whereas the other president might consider the resources adequate. In either case, the president's response sheds light on the relation of resources to mission.

Boggs responded, "Yes, a lack of resources is a problem. In fact, I just left a meeting where we were talking about the need to upgrade our information systems, and we can't figure out how we are going to do that, to generate the resources, so having adequate resources is going to be a continual problem for us." Dassance, while not ranking the lack of resources as a top-rated issue, agreed that limited resources hampered his college's ability to complete its mission adequately. Ku stated, "Yes, I do agree that we do not have adequate resources to fulfill our mission. We are just too short of resources to do the job adequately."

Perkins also stated that a lack of resources restricts his college's ability to complete its mission:

> One of the things I see happening is that the expectations for community colleges are growing. The community is expecting

more from us, the states are expecting more from us, and the resources are not following. So we are in a dilemma. The community college mission is pretty broadly defined, and it's difficult for community college presidents to narrow the mission, that is, to say no to community members and state organizations because although we have seen the rationale for their requests, we don't have adequate resources to meet those requests. As a result, we are trying to do more with less, and it is causing problems for us generally.

Spina likewise acknowledged a lack of resources as a problem in relation to the mission at Monroe Community College. "It is one of the most pressing problems we face. I think we are near the point where we won't have enough resources to accomplish our mission. We are having discussions here about whether we can continue to operate in a comprehensive fashion or whether we need to delete or truncate portions of our mission because the resources aren't there to justify doing a quality job."

Thornley sounded a similar theme: "I do agree that a lack of resources has hampered our mission. . . . Funding for higher education in South Carolina has eroded in the last five years from 93 cents of every dollar that should have been allocated to higher education according to the formula to 66 cents. That's erosion, not perception, but genuine erosion."

Wallace stated that Inver Hills Community College "is substantially underfunded in relation to both need and normative standards within American community colleges."

The presidents who responded "yes" to the question regarding resources and mission were then asked how the mission had been altered at their college as a result of inadequate resources. Boggs noted that at Palomar College they have been unable to employ as many full-time faculty as required and "haven't been able to keep up very well with technology." Noting that keeping abreast of new developments in technology is a problem with most community colleges, Boggs lamented, "We are trying to accomplish our mission the best we can under the circumstances."

Dassance reported that inadequate resources have forced community college leaders to examine their college's mission more carefully and to establish priorities. He noted, "I guess I'd answer the question in a funny way. I think a lack of resources has been a blessing in some ways. I think it has forced community colleges to analyze their mission and decide what the core of the mission is. . . .We've gone through a process of establishing as clearly as we could what our vision for the future is, what our mission is in terms of statutory requirements, and what major strategic directions we were to take. We then tried to build everything around those strategic decisions, prioritizing around the ends we want to achieve." He agreed that today's community college cannot be all things to all people and that one goal of the assessment process, brought on in part due to limited resources, is to cut back or stop doing certain things.

Ku noted that inadequate resources have forced South Seattle Community College to close certain programs and that the college may have to close its heavy equipment programs, such as diesel mechanics, because of a lack of resources. Similarly, Perkins stated that "because of a lack of resources we do not exert as much effort as we once did to develop associate degree programs in the technologies, programs that were once a strong part of the community college's mission. Today, we tend to put more emphasis in those areas that are more cost effective for us."

Spina noted that as a result of inadequate resources to support the college's mission fully, Monroe Community College is feeling the pressure from the faculty:

> At this college, like many others, we have a collegial partnership, and some of our faculty are beginning to question the

kinds of outreach we are doing and the partnerships we are forming with community groups. Faculty members are beginning to question our role with workforce development, workforce preparation, and training. They are saying to us in increasingly pointed ways, "Why are we expanding these programs when we really can't give our students the kind of instructional equipment that they need to compete in a technological world. We are increasing class size at a time when our students need more hands-on work." The faculty are wondering if we can continue to be all things to all people; they feel that we haven't devoted enough attention and resources to our core mission of occupational and transfer education.

Wallace noted that Inver Hills Community College was suffering because the state of Minnesota was cutting back its contribution to community colleges. "Although we feel very strongly about the importance of developmental education, there are minimal resources available to support that element of our mission." Wallace noted that workforce development and other activities associated with economic development are an important part of Inver Hills's mission but "we have received negligible support for that aspect of our mission, thus placing great strain on our ability to function as a comprehensive community college."

Thornley, while stopping short of saying that the mission has been altered as a result of inadequate resources, asked rhetorically, "If you are growing, and we have been, and resources are declining, how do you cope?" Trident Technical College's answer, as has often been the case with community colleges across the nation for more than a decade, has been to increase class size and employ more part-time instructors. But, Thornley noted she didn't think the college could continue doing so without it having an impact on the mission.

As was true with the other presidents, Sanchez observed that the question of mission and resources puts pressure on presidents to explore untapped resources within the college and the community. The question "is a complex one. . . . We need to look at different ways of doing business, and I don't think we have explored fully the use of technology or partnerships with business and industry. I don't think a simple answer like a lack of resources really tells the full story."

Thor believes to some extent that a lack of resources is a major issue facing community colleges in accomplishing their mission, but "only when considering traditional resources. We are seeing more of our resources coming from tuition than from state aid. We are also feeling the pressure from taxpayers who are resisting increases in property taxes. I think, however, that if community colleges act in a more entrepreneurial fashion, those resources can not only be replaced but can be increased." She quickly noted, however, that "we have narrowed our mission over the years. We realized that we needed to narrow our mission to those things that we could do best, to identify our market niche. As a result, we have three areas of focus. . . . We have redirected those resources into those areas of focus of our mission."

Harris asserted that a lack of funds has not adversely hampered Parkland College in fulfilling its mission. Offering a rather comprehensive answer to the question, she explained how Parkland approaches the question of resources and mission, pointing out that the college must establish priorities:

> One of the things we have done is to use a collegewide approach to addressing issues that are directly related to our mission. We bring in folks from the community, and they are told what our mission and purpose are. We then do environmental scanning, and our planning committee takes the data and analyzes them. From that, we identify our strategic goals. As a result, we look at our budget and we link our strategic goals to our budget; our planning committee is responsible for determining what activities, programs, and services we should fund. We utilize this information in driving our budget.
>
> Our process here does not allow a budget process to drive our programs and services; rather, it's the other way around.

We need to continue to do this in order to ensure that we are addressing the major priorities of the college that are consistent with our mission. I don't personally see that money is the major problem facing our college. I think maintaining some entrepreneurial vision and getting people to buy into that vision and utilizing all of the talents that you have so you can address the opportunities and restraints presented is important. This is especially true in the area of technology.

Giles of the Kansas City Metropolitan Community College District adamantly disagrees that a lack of resources has limited the colleges in his district in accomplishing their mission:

I do not agree that a lack of resources restricts our mission. There are 12 community college districts in this state and over the last decade we have spoken with one voice to the state legislature as to the mission of the community college and to the value of the community college. We have worked the state capital to get the types of appropriations from the legislature we need. We are now recognized as a major influence educationally as well as politically. We have become involved in making personal contributions to campaigns to get people elected or reelected who are supportive of the community college. So at the local level we have raised our visibility, raised the image of our community college, and this helps in terms of obtaining contributions.

Wallin noted that "I think at this point we have adequate resources to fulfill our mission, although we don't have adequate resources to be all that the community and our business and industry partners expect us to be. We meet our payrolls, keep our buildings maintained, but we don't have what we need to meet the expectations of our community in terms of technology, expansion, and these sorts of things."

Myran stated that Washtenaw Community College "actually does have adequate resources to fulfill its mission. We are located in a unique area. Since the University of Michigan and

Eastern Michigan University are here, we function in an environment where education is highly supported. . . . However, we have the 'haves' and 'have-nots' in the community college movement. I think that is becoming a serious problem."

In every case, the presidents interviewed are sensitive to the need to obtain adequate resources if their colleges are going to fulfill their mission. The interviewees are involved in a variety of activities that assist in obtaining resources for their colleges, activities that are similar to those that take place in one way or another and to one degree or another on practically every community college campus in the nation.

Myran works hard to see that the voters in Washtenaw's district support millage and bond issues. Giles works very closely with business and industry to obtain funds for a technology center. Sanchez helped his college obtain funds from Intel and other companies to help fund a program in semiconductor manufacturing technology. Thor noted that Arizona has diversified funding sources, laws, and regulations that allow the colleges to be entrepreneurial in obtaining revenue. She takes advantage of the flexibility. Boggs works closely with the legislature. In addition, his college works closely with federal, county, and city leaders to develop joint projects such as a bus transit center and a wellness and fitness center. Perkins is involved with the college's foundation as well as with seeking grant funds from the federal government. Dassance also places major emphasis on raising funds from private sources as well as seeking additional partners to share the cost of college activities. Wallin maintains good relations with the state legislators and county commissioners. She, like most of the other presidents interviewed, seeks help from the private sector, including donors to the foundation.

The presidents interviewed, without exception, do not believe the community college can "be all things to all people." Community colleges have always had restrictions on the number of programs and courses they could offer and the number of people they could serve; nevertheless, until recently some presidents and other community college leaders continued to see the community college as answering all of society's calls. Such idealism will become more difficult to find if the views of the 13 presidents interviewed represent the national mood.

OPEN ACCESS AND THE MISSION

One of the major tenets of the community college's philosophy is a commitment to open access admissions. Open access is closely related to the college's mission; who enrolls at the community college influences what is taught and who benefits from the community college. For example, if community colleges dropped remedial education from their offerings, open access admissions would have to be reinterpreted, as would the college's mission.

Perhaps nothing presidents do is more important than consistently and effectively communicating the mission to the college's numerous constituents. The plaintive cry, "they don't understand us," has been heard in every community college boardroom across the nation at one time or another. Indeed, the interviews contain some references to the community college not being understood by some of its constituents. Everything from funding to enrollment of students depends upon the public's understanding and support of the community college's mission. To communicate the mission effectively, presidents must understand open access as both a philosophical concept and as a practical means of fulfilling the college's mission.

Q: Perhaps the most compelling development in American higher education in this half of the 20th century has been the nation's commitment to open access. At the heart (and in many ways the soul) of the open access movement has been and are the community colleges. How do you define open access?

Do you feel that open access is threatened? If so, what are the threats?

Open access is a complex and often misunderstood concept. For example, it is very difficult to explain to the local Rotary Club why the community college is teaching high school-level or below courses in reading, English, and mathematics. "Why are we, the taxpayer, paying to have this taught twice?" is often the refrain presidents hear when addressing various civic groups; occasionally even members of the college's governing board ask the same question. It is also difficult to explain to high school teachers and guidance counselors how a student who barely scraped by with a C- average in high school and who was often a discipline problem made the community college's dean's list. The answer is that the student is enrolled in auto mechanics at the community college, something he has always loved and is very good at; he also devotes more than 50 hours a week to working with automobiles.

Admitting to the college anyone who is a high school graduate or who is at least 18 years old and can benefit academically from attending the college is the definition of open access that has often found its way into enabling legislation and numerous college catalogs. The definition is useful and necessary for legal as well as technical reasons; yet it cries for further explanation. The presidents interviewed are unwilling to limit their definition of open access, and the practices that sustain it, solely to a technical definition. How, then, do current community college presidents define open access?

Ku began his definition of open access in a somewhat traditional way. He noted that both the governor and the legislature in his state support open access, which means that "anybody who has a high school diploma can come to South Seattle

Community College." He noted, however, that open access has taken on a new dimension at South Seattle since "a lot of immigrants come here to study English as a second language; that is a part of our open access."

Spina too referred to the legal implications of open access: "Open access is actually a legal concept here in New York State. There is a law that states essentially that community colleges are required to accept for full-time study all applicants who graduated from high school in our service area the previous June and all returning veterans who wish to study full time." Moving away from the technical and legal definition, Spina continued, "I look on open access as a concept that allows us to offer opportunities to people who dropped out of high school. We have many people who want to start a college education even though they dropped out of high school two years ago or 20 years ago. So far, the college has been able to make that commitment to open access and stick to it and provide the kinds of services that these students need to be successful."

To Boggs, open access means that higher education "is accessible to anyone who desires to pursue it." He noted that to be accessible, community colleges must be within commuting distance of their students and must offer courses and programs at times that are convenient for students. "We're accessible in that we are flexible enough to allow returning students to come full time or part time. Our schedules are more flexible than many four-year institutions. So access is really at the heart of the community college mission. That's part of what we are all about."

Myran stated that open access means that "the community college is very knowledgeable about its community—the demography of its community—so that it knows what community groups exist and how they fit with the mission of the community college. In other words, open door—open access—should mean more than simply being open to people coming to the campus. It should mean identifying the needs of constituents and being aggressive about recruitment and designing special programs to respond to those needs."

Thor, like Myran, placed responsiveness to the community high on her list of what it means to be an open access institution. She noted that "we operate in approximately 250 locations around Maricopa County, ranging from shopping malls to high schools to churches to corporate conference rooms. We facilitate access in terms of a number of locations where people can receive services. Next, we facilitate access in terms of how we format our schedule. Only 2 to 3 percent of our courses are a semester in length. We also have been pioneering distance learning for almost 20 years." In essence, open access to Thor means "figuring out how to provide the services to the people wherever they are and whenever they can take advantage of what we have."

One of the enduring myths associated with the community college and one growing out of the college's commitment to open access is the misconception that admission to the college means admission to a program of study. As several of the presidents explained, admission to a program of study is not automatic.

Perkins noted that "many of our programs are highly competitive in terms of entrance requirements, so access is really to the college. We then become much more selective in access to our programs; access is based on students' academic backgrounds. Our nursing program, for example, still is quite competitive. Our veterinary technology program is very competitive and is getting more so." Similarly, Giles noted that "my definition is access to the college and not specifically open access to any program. Some programs must continue to have admission standards to get into, whether they be in allied health or some of the technologies." Giles added an important caveat: "If a person doesn't meet those program admission standards, the college has to be ready then to say we have the programs to prepare you so you can meet them." Wallin echoed a similar theme to that of Perkins and Giles. She explained: "We have open admissions to the college. We do not have open admission to all of our programs within the college. We have requirements that may be higher for some of our medical programs, for example. We have programs that might have a higher reading or math level requirement than simply basic entry to the college." She too makes an important additional point regarding access. "In order to accommodate people who may not have those skills, we have an extensive developmental program designed to bring people to the level where they will succeed in college-level work."

Harris believes that defining open access as enrolling anyone "who can benefit" from college attendance is of little help. She thinks essentially anyone could benefit. The problem in defining and implementing open access is determining who can benefit from what. "I tend to believe that the only thing we have available is a series of tests that determine where people can go, whether it's developmental, whether it's continuing education so they can enroll in adult basic education, or whether they can take academic level courses. I think the challenge to open access is that everybody is coming through the door. With that, the real challenge is how can we design programs and services to meet this wide array of needs. That's the challenge: to meet the needs of the public while maintaining the integrity of academic programs."

Sanchez's definition and ensuing discussion of open access also emphasize what happens to students after they are admitted to the college. "Open access? What happens after open access I think is probably the more important question. Does it mean that we just bring them on board? I think we have to focus on student success, not just access. If we define access as just entry into an institution, that's not enough. We have to focus on getting them into the right kinds of programs, finding out, perhaps even helping them to discover, what their goals in life might be. Access needs to go beyond initial access to the college to a continuing access so that students can continue to develop."

Open access, as discussed by the above presidents, certainly means access to additional educational opportunities; it does not mean access to any and every program the college offers nor does it mean that the community college must have something for everyone. On the other hand, open access, if it is to fulfill its promise, means that once a college admits a student, it has an ethical obligation to see that the student has a reasonable chance for academic success.

Threats to Open Access

The presidents interviewed were asked if they perceived any threats to the community college's open access admission policies and, if so, what those threats are. Based upon the above discussions, one threat to open access is a misunderstanding of what it means in practice. Other threats were identified by the presidents interviewed.

As Wallace observed, "The essential element of our mission is open access and, as resources have declined, access has effectively been reduced by our inability to offer as full a program as the demands for our services require. So one element affected has been access." Similarly, Thornley noted that "somebody has to pay the bill. If federally funded programs eliminate the inclusion of remedial programs, then students don't have a way to pay for them regardless of your commitment to remedial students. If your state appropriations eliminate the funding for remedial programs, you don't have a way to provide them." Nevertheless, Thornley noted, "we remain committed to remedial students, as I think most of our colleges do."

Dassance observed that "access is threatened from a number of quarters. I think it is threatened from a changing political climate where state legislatures, and certainly we have seen it in Congress, have become much, much more conservative. I think open access is threatened in a backhand kind of way with our emphasis on performance funding where institutions are being funded based upon completion. There will be a pull toward having those people in the pipeline who are more likely to complete their programs because they are the ones you will be paid for. I see a threat to open access from some of the economic development emphasis and the closer ties we are forming with business and industry, whose leaders may not be tolerant of our philosophical stance on open access."

Myran too spoke about threats to open access emanating from the political environment. "My feeling is that state and federal programs are going to ebb and flow, depending on the political situation, and that more of the local community is going to have to take charge of its own future." Myran described "a more conservative outlook nationally, which is having a negative impact on community colleges. I do sense a change in the mood in the nation."

Perkins discussed some threats to open access beginning to take root among faculty members. He noted that at Blue Ridge Community College a great deal of emphasis is placed on developmental education and the fact that it requires considerable resources. "That, in some ways, has become somewhat problematic for us because I think some of our faculty in particular would like for us to put less emphasis in developmental education and try to find more talented students." Asked if this attitude among faculty toward developmental education is a threat to open access, Perkins replied, "I think it's a potential threat."

Spina is committed to maintaining open access as long as possible. He, like Perkins, pointed out that maintaining open access requires a major commitment of resources to developmental education. He worries, however, that a belief in open access and developmental education "is not shared by our political leaders in New York State—at least not all of them right now—and there are battles brewing in Albany. They don't address the issues of access directly. They take a sort of pusillanimous way of cutting student aid, of instituting standards in the name of quality, for example, instituting standards of completion that require students to complete an associate degree within four years. We all know that is not a realistic completion ratio, especially for our adult students; so by setting completion standards they are limiting access. They don't have the courage to say that is what they are doing, but I'm concerned that these actions threaten open access."

Thor identified rising tuition costs as a way of limiting student access. She also sees employers narrowing the focus of what courses they are willing to fund for their employees. She perceives some things colleges do or do not do as threats to access. "I think failing to be more market sensitive will ultimately threaten access if our colleges do not recognize the need to schedule classes other than between 9:00 A.M. and 10:00 A.M., Monday, Wednesday, and Friday on a 16-week semester."

Developmental education plays an important role in Palomar College's commitment to open access. Boggs believes that "one of the threats to open access is the continual questioning of whether community colleges should be in the business of remedial or developmental education." Boggs noted that to enroll in developmental education, many students need federal student aid, especially Pell Grants. If Pell Grants are denied to developmental students, Boggs believes open access will be threatened, because "for many of our students, access depends upon whether they can get financial assistance." Boggs noted that "if the colleges don't have the resources, they can't offer the classes. Maintaining open access is going to be a real challenge for us, given the financial constraints and the large number of students headed toward higher education."

Those presidents who see cuts in developmental education as a threat to open access can point to recent activities in Alabama to confirm their fears. The *Community College Times* reports that the Alabama Commission on Higher Education (ACHE) proposes cuts of $102 million to higher education, of which $27.5 million would come from community colleges. The cuts would cause community colleges to lose the money set aside for remedial education. As one Alabama community college president noted, ACHE's plan would eliminate completely the concept of open access to higher education. According to the *Times* article, "Many educators [in Alabama] say that this proposal couldn't come at a worse time. Welfare reform has put increasing pressure on states to put public aid recipients to work, but most need training before they qualify for an increasingly complex job market. The plan also jeopardizes the traditional community college 'open door' " (Rucker, 1997, p. 2). Regardless of how the Alabama situation is resolved, open access has been challenged, in at least one state.

The above discussion of open access illustrates that there is more than one way to close the community college's open door. The discussions also reveal that those presidents interviewed understand the importance of open access to the community college's mission, to its students, to higher education in general, to their individual colleges, and to society in general. Open access is a concept and a practice that will require a commitment from community college presidents if it is going to be a cornerstone of the community college philosophy and mission in the future. As suggested by those presidents interviewed and shown in the examples from the *Community College Times*, a number of forces in society are mitigating the nation's commitment to universal higher education. If community colleges do not take a stand, these forces may prevail. Presidents must understand, promote, and defend open access to the nation's community colleges. To do any less is to abort a major tenet of the community college's mission and philosophy and to fail as a community college leader.

EXTERNAL AND INTERNAL INFLUENCES ON THE MISSION

Q: What other outside influences are encroaching upon the college's ability to accomplish its mission, and indeed, to function effectively on a daily basis?

How are you balancing the pressures of these influences with those of the college's mission?

Ku sees no threats either externally or internally to the college's mission or to the college's ability to perform daily tasks. On the other hand, Harris sees both internal and external threats. She stated that the "threat of change internally seems to be the one factor encroaching on our ability to do our job. We have a lot of people who have been here a long time and they just see all of this happening: the changing technology and different types of people coming into their classrooms with different needs. Trying to provide those who have been here with the resources to make them comfortable with all of these changes is really a challenge. It's really an impediment to achieving our mission." For Harris, the only external threat is "a lack of true understanding of the mission of the community college, especially at the legislative level."

Thornley pointed to major changes taking place in South Carolina, especially in the way public community technical colleges are funded. "In South Carolina we are transforming from formula-driven funding by the state to performance-driven funding. There is a sense that colleges have waste and duplication, that business and industry were required to downsize and colleges never did. To a great extent, we have invited the scrutiny that comes from legislatures who have decided that they don't really need to put more money into higher education; they just need to reshuffle what is there." She continued by noting that the community college presidents in her state must demonstrate that the colleges operate efficiently or face the legislature:

> I think legislators will be intrusive on our ability to meet our mission. They will be intrusive under the umbrella of accountability. So in a nutshell, my concern is a legislature looking for easy answers to very complex issues. People of influence and people in the legislature, at least in South Carolina, were educated in venues other than the two-year college. They don't quite understand who we are and what we do. Sometimes they don't have a clue about what we do at Trident Technical College and because they don't have a clue, they can't appreciate what our mission is.

Myran pointed out that "certainly a national trend, not so much at WCC, is the movement toward more activist boards of trustees. Board members are, in effect, concluding that educators by themselves—faculty and administrators—will not be cost effective, that they will not be productive, and they will not be accountable. Trustees watch the resources and therefore are starting to take charge themselves. So I think the challenge for us as educators is to take charge of our future and to reassure our governing boards that we are willing to be held accountable. I would say that is the greatest threat: this loss of confidence in educators in managing their affairs and shaping the best future."

Thor reinforced Myran's observations:

> We have recently had a change on our board. For the first time in a long time we are seeing split votes on our board. We have a board member who is a recent graduate of one of our col-

leges and a board that is more inclined to listen to dissident voices and anonymous letters. As a president in the system I find that my energies are devoted more and more to addressing some of those kinds of things instead of what I perceive to be a higher calling. So the board is definitely a force. I also think there is increasing pressure from minority groups. We are also seeing forces within the legislature here in Arizona who are interested in privatization, increasing competition, and who are basically suspicious of public institutions and how they use their funds. So we have a lot that is distracting our attention from what I would consider to be our main mission.

Perkins, while clarifying that his college has only minor problems with outside influence and internal conflicts regarding the community college's mission, noted that the state-level coordinating body for higher education in Virginia has criticized institutions of higher education in the state, thus "making it more difficult for individual presidents to work autonomously for the benefit of their communities." Returning to a theme he commented on earlier regarding questioning of the mission by the faculty, he noted that "some of the faculty are feeling that their credit programs are being threatened because students enroll in noncredit workshops to get what they need, rather than enrolling in credit courses. So there is a division at the college between those who promote and develop noncredit and those who promote and develop our credit offerings. I see it as healthy, and while I do not see it as a threat, I see it as an issue that we need to resolve as a college."

Spina praised his college board and all of the stakeholders associated with the college. He noted, however, that "the real threats, the real difficulties that we have had with reaching our mission's goals, have come from external funding. In our community we have a population that is aging, the young people are leaving us, and the aging population does not want to pay more taxes. Politicians are responding by cutting public spending; thus, the spending levels from the state have decreased." He also noted that "internally we have problems. When money gets tight, some faculty have a tendency to circle the wagons under the rubric of bringing us back to our core mission, which means that we should be accommodating only transfer, liberal arts, and high-end vocational programs. Those faculty members feel that we ought to be cutting back on workforce training and economic development. Even remedial work comes under attack sometimes by some of our faculty who wish to have the college resemble what it was in the 1960s when the students were arguably better prepared, better motivated."

Wallace noted that although the mission at Inver Hills is essentially unchanged, the "political, regulatory, and administrative environment we operate in has changed dramatically." He noted that legislators expect higher levels of accountability and cost effectiveness along with "reduced financial allocations." As is true with other presidents interviewed, Wallace noted that the college has "encountered a great deal of resistance to the kinds of change that will be necessary" if the college is to function effectively in meeting the demands of the new economy.

Giles praised his board for its support and its service to the community. He did not point to any internal impediments to achieving the system's mission. He does feel, however, that "the actions of state legislators—some of the actions they take, some of the laws they pass, some of the restrictions they put on some of our appropriations—are interfering in how we respond to our community."

Sanchez suggested that one can take external intrusions into the affairs of the college in one of two ways: "Are board members encroaching or can that be turned into something that is helpful and useful to the community college? By working with them, a number of presidents have been able to turn board members around to where they are now dealing with the issues that are important to community colleges." All is not perfect, however. He noted that state coordinating boards, the federal government, accrediting bodies, and other organizations demand too much information. Gathering the information takes time and energy away from the college's ability to reach its goals.

CONCLUDING REMARKS

It is apparent from the interviews that the presidents are committed to open access as an important part of the community college philosophy, although none of the presidents interviewed interpret open access to mean that the community college can or should be all things to all people. For the most part, even though there are some internal and external threats to open access, they feel it will be preserved, even though resources are more scarce than several of the presidents would like. The presidents interviewed, without exception, understand the community college mission and the need to communicate that mission effectively and efficiently to the colleges' various constituents. All of the presidents interviewed seem excited about the prospects of leading the community college in these times of great change.

5

◆

WOMEN AND MINORITIES IN THE COMMUNITY COLLEGE PRESIDENCY

The community college embodies many of the democratic ideals within American society. Through its commitment to open admissions access, the community college embraces the values of inclusion, diversity, and egalitarianism. People from all walks of life are encouraged to improve their personal, professional, and economic conditions by attending the community college. As stated by one president, "There is no better place to celebrate the convergence of cultures than to look at [community college] students; . . . to reflect those students in the staff, the faculty, and the administration and to celebrate how that reflection is a microcosm of American society" (J. S. Owens, quoted in Gillett-Karam, Roueche, & Roueche, 1991, p. 180).

Does the community college reflect the changing demographic profile of the United States? In 1990, the total resident population in the United States was approximately 51 percent female. Population projections for the 21st century indicate that the proportion of male and female residents will continue to be approximately equal (Department of Commerce, 1996). Between 1980 and 1990, the percentage increase in minority populations far exceeded the increase in the Caucasian population. In 1995, the United States population had the following composition: 74 percent non-Hispanic Caucasian, 13 percent African American, 10 percent Hispanic, 4 percent Asian American/Pacific Islander, and one percent Native American/ Eskimo/Aleut (Riche, 1996). It is estimated that minorities will constitute 50 percent of the nation's population by the year 2030. By the year 2000, minorities are expected to be in the majority in 53 of America's largest cities (Rendon & Valadez, 1994).

The community college's student population contains a percentage of minorities and women similar to that found in the general public. In 1991, minority students constituted more than 25 percent of community college enrollments nationwide, and approximately 58 percent of all community college students were women (Cohen & Brawer, 1996).

The academic success of female and minority students within and beyond the community college influences the availability of women and minorities for positions of academic leadership. For example, if minority students do not continue their education beyond the associate degree and earn the appropriate terminal degree or doctorate, then "the pool of minority group members [for faculty positions] is limited while a sustained volume of Caucasian candidates continues" (Blackwell, 1988, p. 419). And, since most minority academic administrators come through the faculty pipeline (Wilson, 1996), fewer minority faculty means fewer minority academic administrators.

Women have greater representation on the faculty of community colleges than do minorities. In 1991, more than 43 percent of the faculty were female (Townsend, 1996) and in 1989–90, approximately 10 percent were minorities (Carter, 1994). Women, however, are still underrepresented in top administrative levels. In a 1989 study of academic deans (Vaughan, 1990), 21 percent of the 619 chief academic officers who responded to the survey were women and 7 percent were minorities.

Since most community college presidents are promoted into the presidency from the chief academic officer's position (Boggs, 1988; Vaughan, 1986, 1996), a paucity of female and minority academic administrators translates into a paucity of female and minority presidential candidates. Therefore, as both educator and employer, the community college plays an important role in influencing how well women and minorities are represented in the community college presidency.

This chapter focuses on women and minorities who have reached the community college presidency. The characteristics of female and minority presidents, their comparison to male and Caucasian presidents, and strategies for improving the percentage of women and minorities in the presidency are discussed. Survey results and interview responses are presented.

FEMALE AND MINORITY PRESIDENTS TODAY

Demographic Characteristics

Throughout this book, the categories of gender and race or ethnicity are not considered to be mutually exclusive. When statistics about women are presented, these numbers include all women, regardless of race or ethnicity. Likewise, when statistics regarding minority presidents are presented, the figures represent both female and male minorities. In this chapter, some of the data are further divided. The responses from the 1996 CLS are subdivided by race or ethnicity (Caucasian or minority) and by gender (male or female). Thus, for each characteristic presented, the responses from Caucasian male presidents, Caucasian female presidents, minority male presidents, and minority female presidents are provided separately. Due to rounding, actual column totals may vary slightly from 100 percent.

Gender and Race or Ethnicity.[1] Of the presidents responding to the survey in 1996, 18 percent are women and 82 percent are men. Seventy-two percent are Caucasian men, 14 percent are Caucasian women, 10 percent are minority men, and 4 percent are minority women. Of the 553 men, 88 percent are Caucasian and 12 percent are minority. Of the 119 women, 77 percent are Caucasian and 24 percent are minority. (See Table 5.1 for a breakdown of all presidents by gender and race or ethnicity.)

Current Age. Presidents were asked to state their age at their last birthday. In general, regardless of race or ethnicity, current female presidents are younger than male presidents, and minority presidents are younger than Caucasian presidents. The average age of all community college presidents is 55 years old. The average age of Caucasian male presidents is 55 years old; the average age of Caucasian female presidents is 51 years old; the average age of minority male presidents is 54 years old; and the average age of minority female presidents is 52 years old. (See Table 5.2 for the age ranges of community college presidents.)

Table 5.1 Presidents by Gender and Race or Ethnicity

	Male *n*=553	Female *n*=119
Caucasian	88%	77%
Minority	12%	24%
Total	100%	100%

---

1. Presidents were given the following categories from which to select when identifying their race or ethnicity: American Indian/Native American, Asian American/Pacific Islander, African American, Hispanic, White/Caucasian, and Other. (Presidents were asked to select only one category of race or ethnicity.) Throughout the book, the term *minority* is used for all presidents who selected categories other than White/Caucasian.

Table 5.2   Current Age of Presidents

	Caucasian Male *n*=483	Caucasian Female *n*=91	Minority Male *n*=68	Minority Female *n*=27
Under 40 years old	<1%	0%	<1%	0%
40–49 years old	14%	43%	24%	33%
50–59 years old	67%	51%	52%	63%
60 years or older	19%	6%	22%	4%
Total	100%	100%	100%	100%

Attaining the Presidency

Current Position. On the average, Caucasian male presidents have been in their current position nearly twice as long as all other presidents. Minority female presidents, on the average, have been in their current position for the shortest period of time. The average number of years that Caucasian men have been in their current position is 8.7 years; Caucasian female presidents have been in their current position for 4.3 years. The average number of years that minority men have been in their current position is 4.9 years, and minority female presidents have been in their current position for 3.4 years.

Average Presidential Tenure. The presidents were asked to report the total number of years that they have served as a community college president. As with the number of years in their position, Caucasian male presidents have the longest average presidential tenure, followed relatively closely be minority male presidents. Minority female presidents currently have the shortest presidential tenure. (See Table 5.3.)

Table 5.3   Average Presidential Tenure (in Years)

	Caucasian Male	Caucasian Female	Minority Male	Minority Female	All Presidents
Average presidential tenure	11.2	5.3	8.7	4.0	9.8

Number of Presidencies. The majority of all presidents are in their first presidency. Nearly three-fourths of the Caucasian male, Caucasian female, and minority female presidents and approximately one-half of the minority male presidents are in their first presidency. Of the minority female presidents who responded to the survey question, all were in their first or second presidency. Similarly, 92 percent of the Caucasian female presidents were in their first or second presidency. Male presidents have had up to five presidencies, although 96 percent of the Caucasian male presidents and 91 percent of the minority male presidents have had between one and three presidencies.

Age at First Presidency. The average age at which all presidents assumed their first presidency was approximately 44 years old. Women assumed their first presidency at a later age than did men. The average age at which Caucasian men assumed their first presidency was approximately 43.7 years old; the average age at which Caucasian women assumed their first presidency was 46.3 years old; the average age at which minority men assumed their first presidency was 45 years old, and the average age at which minority women assumed their presidency was 47.3 years old. Table 5.4 shows the age ranges at which all presidents assumed their first presidency.

Table 5.4   Age at First Presidency

	Caucasian Male *n*=479	Caucasian Female *n*=90	Minority Male *n*=68	Minority Female *n*=26
Under 40 years old	29%	14%	21%	8%
40–49 years old	52%	58%	57%	58%
50–59 years old	19%	27%	19%	35%
60 years or older	<1%	1%	3%	0%
Total	100%	100%	100%	100%

Position Held Before First Presidency

The chief academic officer position is the most commonly held position by all presidents before their first presidency. More than 50 percent of the Caucasian male presidents and Caucasian female presidents were in positions with academic overview before their first presidencies. To a slightly lesser degree (just under 50 percent), minority male presidents and minority female presidents occupied positions with academic overview before their first presidency. The chief student services officer was the next most common position held by all presidents before their first presidency, with 6 percent of the Caucasian male presidents, 10 percent of the Caucasian female presidents, 10 percent of the minority male presidents, and 14 percent of the minority female presidents holding this position before their first presidency.

Community college boards prefer presidential candidates who have had previous experience as a president. When asked whom they would select for president among candidates currently employed in a variety of positions, more than 75 percent stated that their first choice would be a president from another community college (Vaughan & Weisman, 1997, p. 147). When boards cannot or do not hire a sitting president, they may decide to hire from within their institution. It appears that neither gender nor race or ethnicity has a bearing on selecting an internal candidate for a presidency. Approximately 33 percent of the Caucasian male presidents, 32 percent of the Caucasian female presidents, 30 percent of the minority male presidents, and 32 percent of the minority female presidents were internal candidates when they assumed their first presidency.

Perceptions about the Position

Time on the Job. Presidents were asked to state the number of hours they spent performing the duties associated with the presidency on a weekly basis. Caucasian female presidents and minority female presidents reported a slightly higher average number of hours worked per week than did their male counterparts. Table 5.5 presents the average reported hours per week spent on duties associated with the presidency for Caucasian male, Caucasian female, minority male, minority female, and all presidents.

Table 5.5　Average Reported Hours per Week Spent Performing Presidential Duties

	Caucasian Male	Caucasian Female	Minority Male	Minority Female	All Presidents
Average reported weekly hours	56.7	60.9	55.8	58.9	57.2

Perceptions of Stress. According to the responses to the survey, Caucasian male presidents are evenly split between those who rate the presidency as a high-stress position and those who rate it as a moderate-stress position. In all other groups, more presidents perceive the presidency to be a position of high stress than one of moderate stress. Minority female presidents have the highest percentage of responses that rate the presidency as a high-stress position; however, they also have the highest percentage of responses that rate the presidency as a low-stress position. (See Table 5.6 for the presidents' ratings of stress associated with the presidency.)

Perceptions of Risk. Presidents' perceptions of risk associated with the presidency differs somewhat from their perceptions of stress. Again, minority female presidents have the highest percentage of responses that rate the presidency as a high-risk position, and they also have the highest percentage of responses that rate the presidency as a low-risk position. Caucasian male presidents have the lowest percentage of responses in the high-risk category. (See Table 5.7.)

Table 5.6   Perception of Stress Associated with the Presidency

	Caucasian Male *n*=478	Caucasian Female *n*=90	Minority Male *n*=68	Minority Female *n*=27
High stress	50%	61%	52%	67%
Moderate stress	49%	37%	46%	26%
Low stress	1%	2%	3%	7%
Total	100%	100%	100%	100%

Table 5.7   Perception of Risk Associated with the Presidency

	Caucasian Male *n*=477	Caucasian Female *n*=91	Minority Male *n*=69	Minority Female *n*=27
High risk	36%	48%	52%	56%
Moderate risk	57%	51%	48%	30%
Low risk	7%	1%	0%	14%
Total	100%	100%	100%	100%

Leaving the Position

Moving to Another Position. Presidents were asked how likely they are to seek or accept another full-time position within the next five years. Caucasian male presidents are the least likely to seek or accept another position within the next five years and minority female presidents are the most likely to seek or accept another position within the next five years. (See Table 5.8.)

Presidents were asked if they are likely to move, and what position they would be interested in seeking or accepting. The overwhelming response by all presidents was to continue in community college administration. Of the 303 presidents who stated that it is likely they will seek or accept another position within the next five years, 73 percent stated they are interested in obtaining another community college presidency. Of those interested in seeking another presidency, 65 percent are Caucasian men, 20 percent are Caucasian women, 10 percent are minority men, and 5 percent are minority women.

The chancellorship of a state community college system was identified by six percent of the 303 presidents who stated that it is likely they will seek or accept another position within the

Table 5.8 Likelihood of Presidents Seeking or Accepting
Another Position within the Next Five Years

	Caucasian Male n=480	Caucasian Female n=89	Minority Male n=69	Minority Female n=27
Very likely	18%	28%	28%	48%
Somewhat likely	23%	28%	23%	19%
Not likely	59%	44%	49%	33%
Total	100%	100%	100%	100%

next five years. Of these presidents, 69 percent are Caucasian men, 19 percent are minority men, and 12 percent are minority women. No Caucasian women stated that they will seek or accept a state system chancellorship.

Retirement. Presidents were asked in how many years they plan to retire. Caucasian male presidents are more likely than any other group to retire within one to six years, followed by minority male presidents, minority female presidents, and Caucasian female presidents. (See Table 5.9.)

Regardless of whether presidents move to a new position or retire on a voluntary or involuntary basis, the result is a vacant presidential position that needs to be filled. Between 1991 and 1995, the percentage of community college presidential positions that were vacant each year ranged between 10 and 14 percent (Vaughan, 1996). In addition, approximately 79 percent of current presidents plan to move to another position or retire within the next six years, The following section addresses questions related to filling these vacant positions.

Table 5.9 Presidents' Plans to Retire

	Caucasian Male *n*=473	Caucasian Female *n*=99	Minority Male *n*=67	Minority Female *n*=28
1–3 years	22%	6%	12%	4%
4–6 years	27%	26%	28%	29%
7–10 years	23%	21%	24%	32%
10 or more years	29%	48%	36%	36%
Total	100%	100%	100%	100%

INCREASING REPRESENTATION OF WOMEN AND MINORITIES IN THE PRESIDENCY

The 13 interviewees were asked a number of questions regarding women's and minorities' standing in the presidency. (See chapter 4 for a list of the presidents interviewed.)

The Current Ratio

Q: More than 85 percent of the current community college presidents are Caucasian and approximately 82 percent are male. Do you feel that community college leaders should exert more effort to prepare and recruit minority (defined as non-Caucasian) and female presidents?

If yes, what role do current presidents play in preparing future presidents? What are you doing to prepare minorities and women for the presidency?

If no, why do you feel that more minority and women presidents are not needed?

Some of the interviewees were surprised at the figures that showed more than 85 percent of the current presidents are Caucasian and approximately 82 percent are male. Wallace commented,

> I think community colleges have always drawn great strength from diversity and will continue to do so in the future. In my work with community college leaders across the country, I know that diversity, particularly in the leadership branch, is a very high value. I have seen a lot of commitment to improving leadership diversity among other community college leaders, and I see it as a strong current and sustained value.

All presidents interviewed stated that they believed that more women and minorities should be in the presidency. When asked, they all agreed that community college leaders should exert more effort to prepare and recruit minority and female presidents. The following quotes reflect compelling arguments provided by the presidents for preparing and recruiting more women and minorities for the presidency:

> I think we have an obligation to help all qualified individuals become prepared to lead our community colleges. In the next 10 years, there are going to be a lot of Caucasian male presidents leaving. I think we have an obligation to develop the new emerging leadership and I think we have an extra obligation to bring individuals who represent the students that we serve or the communities that we serve into the mainstream (Perkins).

> We need to increase the percentage of women and minorities in the presidency because the population for the next century is not going to be all Caucasian male (Ku).

> We need to be sensitive to the needs of the people that we serve, and certainly one of the sensitivities is to provide them not only with faculty but with administrative leadership that reflects the general qualities of the population. . . . It certainly

seems reasonable to me that if 85 percent or 82 percent are either Caucasians or males, that we need to have more diversity in our leadership population (Spina).

The presidents shared the perception that opportunities are improving for female and minority professionals interested in ascending to the presidency. In particular, one president identified what she felt were two factors that contributed to the increasing numbers of women and minority presidents: more women and minorities in the pipeline and more sophisticated and better informed boards.

I think we are getting more and more women and minorities into the pipeline and more and more of them are being hired into the presidency. I think as boards begin to look for good leadership, they are not going to rely on their own network as they used to. I think current boards are more sophisticated than they used to be because the issues are sophisticated—at least the challenges are—and so boards now are learning what their institutional needs are and they are trying to match those needs more effectively with the applicant pool. For example, when I was hired, there were several things they were looking for: a healer, number one; somebody who had had the experience of taking a college that had been in turmoil and moving beyond it; and somebody to do more outreach to the community and truly implement the mission of the community college. The board knew what they wanted and they hired a good consulting firm to help them find what they were looking for. When boards know their institutional needs and seek candidates who meet those needs, they get over the issue of race or gender. Boards really want what is best for their institution, and as they begin to identify their needs to move the institution forward, I think you are going to see more women and people of color getting these type jobs. So with these two factors, more women and minorities in the pipeline and more sophisticated boards, I think you are going to see more and more of us in presidential positions (Harris).

Concern by the presidents was voiced, however, regarding the debate over affirmative action. "The wind is blowing in a different direction in California, reflecting some people's opinion that we do not have to work too hard for diversity now," cautioned one president interviewed. All presidents interviewed saw the need to keep the momentum of increasing representation of women and minorities in the presidency moving forward. One example of a college's effort to institutionalize affirmative action was described by Wallace:

> Inver Hills has a full-time diversity coordinator who works very closely with our human resources office, and we have approached the issue of increasing particularly the diversity in our professional categories of employment through much more aggressive recruitment efforts. Our strategy has been to try to optimize the number of qualified women and minorities in our applicant pools.

Achieving diversity in community college leadership requires more than a commitment; it requires action. To be successful, diversity plans should not stop at the recruitment effort, but should also include retention and promotion of women and minorities (Phelps & Taber, 1996). A first step in achieving gender and racial or ethnic diversity is, however, the recruitment and selection process. The next section explores the role of the board and the president in this process.

The Work of the Board: Selecting the President

Perhaps the most important responsibility of the community college governing board is selecting the college's president. Regardless of the pool of candidates, the board makes the final decision on who becomes president. Current community college trustees tend to mirror the demographic characteristics of current community college presidents. Approximately 87 percent of the trustees are Caucasian and approximately 67 percent are male (CTS)[2]. Does the composition of the board determine the gender or race or ethnicity of the candidate who is selected for the presidency? Although a causal relationship has not been studied and is certainly beyond the scope of the research conducted for this book, it is likely that the board's demographic makeup has an influence on the selection of the president.

Suggestions that trustees should come from diverse backgrounds have been presented for more than half a century (see, for example, Hughes, 1945; Keeton, 1977; Pray, 1975; Rauh, 1969; Vaughan & Weisman, 1997), and the percentage of female and minority trustees has, indeed, increased in the last three decades. In 1969, women constituted 15 percent of the trustees (Rauh, 1969); in 1995, this percentage had more than doubled to 33 percent (CTS). Representation by minorities on community college governing boards increased from approximately 2 percent in 1969 (Rauh, 1969) to 13 percent in 1995 (CTS). Therefore, the composition of community college governing boards is becoming more diverse.

What factors might inhibit a board—even a diverse board—from selecting female or minority presidents? Phelps and Taber (1996) point to the concept of "fit." They state that community college boards are reluctant to hire women or minorities for fear that these candidates would not be accepted by the college community, especially if the staff, faculty, and students are predominantly Caucasian. Further, Phelps and Taber reinforce the concern of one of the presidents interviewed for this study who lamented that some people believe that if their service area

---

2. Unless otherwise noted, the trustee information in this chapter is taken from a national study of 618 community college trustees and 299 presidents conducted by the authors in 1995. Data from the trustees' responses are cited as CTS; data from the presidents' responses are cited as PS. Interview responses from 15 trustees are cited as TI and from 10 presidents as PI.

population is not diverse, then presidents do not have a responsibility to pursue diversity in community college leadership.

Gillett-Karam, et al. (1991) identify some sociological processes that prevent groups or organizations from diversifying their membership. The most overt process is what they refer to as position perfection. An example of position perfection would be boards using criteria that relate primarily to characteristics of the dominant group and that assess underrepresented groups as inferior. Many affirmative action and equal employment opportunity initiatives within community colleges attempt to rectify position perfection. Still, when position requirements focus on traditional knowledge, skills, and experience, Caucasian men may have an edge on being considered the "most qualified candidates."

Two other processes are less obvious, and in some ways, more insidious than position perfection. When a culture of conformity exists within an organization—or, for that matter, within a governing board—the group either consciously or unconsciously commits to maintaining the status quo through emulation of the previous leaders. The phenomenon of selection of sameness (or reproduction of self) is manifested when boards choose candidates with the same characteristics as the individuals conducting the selection.

Widmer (1987) states that boards must struggle with their own understanding of diversity before they can effectively make a commitment to diversity:

> If agencies and their boards are to work successfully toward diversity, they must believe that diversity is important. Almost all board members speak of diversity as a good thing—a beneficial, fair, helpful, noble thing to achieve. But when board members are asked why diversity is good, many are not sure or cannot say. . . . Before boards of directors and individual board members can or will work toward diversity, they must find their own answers to some very difficult questions: Is diversity

important? Why? What kind of diversity? What are the benefits of diversity for the organization, the board, the board member? Should achieving diversity be a priority? Why? (pp. 42-43).

Assuming that boards accept fully the value of diversity and make a commitment to an inclusive presidential recruitment process, what can current presidents do to ensure that more women and minorities are in the presidential pipeline? The interviews with the presidents suggest that the first step might be to clarify the components of the presidential pipeline.

Improving the Odds: Rethinking Access to the Pipeline

Although the most common pathway to the presidency is through academic administration, holding a chief academic officer position is not the only important strategy for aspiring presidents. Qualities that trustees look for in presidents include understanding the mission and being able to translate that understanding into a vision for the institution, having the leadership skills to help the college achieve that vision, having effective communication skills, having knowledge of the community and the relationship between the college and the community, and having experience within the community college field (TI). What can women or minorities do to make themselves competitive for the presidency?

Gaining access to the presidential pipeline may need to be understood as more than attaining a position as a chief academic officer within a community college. Gaining access to the pipeline usually requires holding a doctorate, establishing oneself as a leader within one's community college, and understanding the college from a broad perspective. Although the primary burden falls on the shoulders of the aspiring president, sitting presidents can help aspiring presidents obtain valuable professional development experiences to become competitive for a presidency. First and foremost, presidents can encourage aspiring presidents to obtain a doctorate. Presidents can also support aspiring presidents by arranging for or endorsing professional development activities such as completing an internship with a president, participating in an executive leadership development program, or working on special projects at the senior administrative level.

Doctoral Degree. Although some senior administrative community college positions may be filled by individuals whose highest degree is a master's degree, the majority of senior administrative positions require that applicants hold a doctorate. Therefore, as an important credential for those aspiring to positions that report to the president, a doctorate, in practical terms, is a prerequisite to entering the presidential pipeline.

The opportunities for obtaining a doctorate in higher education administration, and even community college administration, are readily available. Graduate-level course work in higher education administration is offered at approximately 17 percent of the graduate school programs in the United States, and more than half of them provide specialized degrees or specializations in community college education (Lumsden & Stewart, 1992). Of the current community college presidents who hold a doctorate, 62 percent majored in higher education and another 14.5 percent majored in other areas of education: vocational education (3.5 percent) adult education (2.5 percent) or another specialization within education (8.5 percent). The remaining 23.5 percent earned their doctorates in another field or discipline. Therefore, whereas the broad field of education has been the area of study for the majority of community college presidents, it is not a required field of study.

Presidents also expressed the value of earning a doctorate and see it as a major factor in entering the presidential pipeline.

From Alex Sanchez came the following:

> I think we could be looking at what some of the professors of higher education at universities are doing. My question would be, what are they doing to bring women and minorities into doctoral programs and the pipeline so that we have adequate representation from currently underrepresented groups?

Support of formal education is just one of the ways in which presidents can fulfill their responsibility to increase the numbers of women and minorities in the presidential pipeline. Presidents can promote formal education through a number of strategies: helping to establish educational leave or tuition reimbursement programs for faculty and administrators, encouraging women and minorities to seek a doctorate, and recognizing the educational achievement of those who have earned their doctoral degree.

Mentoring. Mentoring was an important way in which the presidents who were interviewed stated that they helped prepare women and minorities for the presidency. The presidents interviewed acted as mentors by developing and offering internships and other opportunities for women and minorities to gain exposure to the many functions inherent in the presidency. Mentoring has been cited as the most important factor in career development (Capozzoli, 1989) and is a proactive strategy for developing successful female and minority leaders.

The following quotes describe the actions that the presidents interviewed have taken in providing mentoring to women and minorities:

> My office has set up an administrative internship program in this district over the past two years. One Hispanic woman recently left here and moved into an associate dean's position at one of our campuses to begin her career in administration.

This coming year we will have an African American woman in that position in my office as an administrative intern. We are doing similar things out on our campuses by getting women and minorities into entry level administrative positions. An associate vice chancellor who reports directly to me was really the major mentor for these interns, but I do get involved with them and get them involved in some state-level things to broaden their experience (Giles).

I have always mentored, from very early on in my career. As a matter of fact, I just had a call from someone whom I had mentored to report to me that she has just been selected for a presidency out in California (Sanchez).

One of my campus directors is a member of a minority group, and I am creating opportunities for him to have the kinds of experiences that could prepare somebody to go on and be a president. He needs to get his doctorate, but I personally am working to provide him with daily experiences that a president would need plus professional growth experiences that would make attaining a presidency possible (Thornley).

We have several state organizations that regularly spend time here at the college and visit with me because many of their members are aspiring either to vice presidencies or presidencies. I spend a considerable amount of time with those groups and with individuals as well. For example, I have provided shadowing experiences for people who are in graduate and professional development programs (Wallin).

Professional Development. Professional development programs help fill in the gaps in experience of those aspiring to the presidency for those who do not have direct work experience at the senior administrative level. Examples of professional development programs for future presidents include the American Association of Community College's Presidential Leadership Workshops, the American Council on Education's Fellows Program, the League for Innovation in the Community

College's Executive Leadership Institute, the Consortium of Community College Development's Leadership Institute, and the Association of Community College Trustees' professional development program for aspiring presidents.

Some professional development programs focus on leadership development specifically for women and minorities: the National Institute for Leadership Development (NILD), the National Council on Black American Affairs's Mentoring Leaders for the Future, the League for Innovation in the Community College's Expanding Leadership Diversity in Community Colleges, the HERS Summer Institute for Women in Higher Education Administration, and the Asilomar Leadership Skills Seminar for Women on the Move. (See Laden, 1996, and Pierce, Mahoney, and Kee, 1996, for a description of these programs.)

The presidents interviewed recognized the value of female and minority participation in professional development programs. Stated Gundar Myran, "I personally try to support professional development, such as the women's scholarship program and the women's leadership development program." Peter Spina described his commitment to sponsoring women and minorities for attending professional development programs:

As a member of the League for Innovation, we have a partnership with the Kellogg Foundation and a couple of other groups to do executive leadership training, and we are looking to make sure we have balanced classes in our executive leadership program. I have recommended every year that at least one and sometimes two of our administrators from Monroe Community College attend the NILD program at Maricopa Community College, the leadership program for women. For 15 years or more I have had women attend that program, and some of them have ascended to leadership roles here. I have also hired a couple of women who graduated from that program. I have three vice-presidents and two of them are women and have received training from that program.

Also, in terms of affirmative action, I have identified some young people of color and I am mentoring them personally to prepare them for leadership roles. I have sent one of them to the League's executive leadership training program this summer out in California. I see him as being a future chief executive officer—I hope here, but if not, somewhere else.

Leadership Experience. Providing increasingly responsible work experiences for women and minorities was a strategy identified by the presidents interviewed to expand the emerging leaders' administrative and leadership experience. Internships or shadowing programs provide emerging leaders with opportunities to experience first-hand aspects of senior-level community college administration:

> We have been a part of a leadership development program that has primarily focused on women and minorities who are in mid-level management, to try to put them through a year's mentoring kind of program. The other thing we will do here in the future is create a kind of possibility for women and minorities especially to gain actual experience working with people who are in upper level management (Dassance).

> I think there is a great deal of work that needs to be done in providing women and minorities with leadership experiences. Part of that, of course, lies far back in terms of helping young women and minorities aspire to those sorts of positions. Much of this kind of career counseling needs to occur back in the elementary and the secondary schools before they begin on a non-administrative career track. Certainly, even if they get on that non-administrative career track—and it certainly was the case with me—through leadership experiences, they may discover that they can be as successful on the administrative side (Wallin).

The presidents interviewed hired women and minorities in senior administrative positions. These appointments position women and minorities for selection as presidents.

I am happy to report that several of my former vice presidents are now presidents at other community colleges. I take great pride in seeing that people whom I have tried to help have moved into presidencies (Boggs).

We have had a lot of success in bringing women into leadership positions at the college. Our administration is approximately 50 percent female and our faculty is more than 50 percent female, so I think we have done a good job with bringing women into key positions at the college. On our faculty we have worked hard to make sure that they are in key leadership positions and have an opportunity, if they wish, to advance into administrative positions (Perkins).

Presidents can have a profound impact on presidential selection through their contact and orientation of the board and by working with emerging community college leaders. As the primary provider of information and orientation to community college governing board members, presidents can work with boards to clarify their values regarding diversity and to understand the importance of opening leadership positions to women and minorities. In addition, presidents recommend others for presidential positions, which may be the single most important act in opening up opportunities for women and minorities to become presidents.

Presidents can also work with college staff to ensure that appropriate recruitment, retention, and promotional programs are developed to include under-represented groups. In addition, they can hire women and minorities for significant leadership positions. Presidents can also institute cross-training, internships, internal sabbaticals, and other programs to provide qualified women and minorities with work experiences that make them more competitive for presidential positions.

The comments made by the presidents who were interviewed showed their commitment to achieving diversity in the community college presidency. Unfortunately, commitment and good intentions do not always guarantee that a goal will be achieved. During the discussion of female and minority presidents, some of the presidents interviewed expressed frustration in not achieving the goals toward which they had aimed. The following responses reveal the frustrations of committed community college presidents who believe in and work toward greater representation of women and minorities in the presidency:

> I have to say that due to the area that we serve, I have not had a lot of success bringing minorities into the pipeline and that has been a frustration. Our minority population is pretty small—we are a rural college in an area that is 95 percent Caucasian. Bringing minorities into the pipeline has been very difficult for us. We really have not done a good job at our college (Perkins).

> I am trying to mentor quite a few minorities, particularly administrators. I have not been very successful for some reason, perhaps because we do not have a strong program at the [local university] and the college does not have a strong connection with the university. I find I need some kind of connection with a university such as the University at Austin, Texas. We have participated in a couple of programs there, but the university is so far away. I am trying to encourage a lot of people of color; I try, but I have not been too successful at this point (Ku).

> I think one of the things that concerns sitting female presidents, and we have met periodically at regional and national meetings to talk about this, is that we do not see that women in dean and vice-president positions right now who are particularly interested in assuming the presidency. They look at the very short tenure of a president as well as the great stresses and pressures that are placed on them and they say to themselves, "I am successful and reasonably well compensated at a dean or vice-president level; why should I do this?" I think this is a real problem; I think more needs to be done to encourage women to consider the presidency as an option but also more needs to

be done to help all presidents, not just women, but men and women, deal more successfully with the conflicts and the stresses of the job. Certainly, I think probably these same things are true for minority administrators who either are not being encouraged into presidencies or do not see it as a plum position any more (Thor).

Despite the frustrations, the presidents interviewed were optimistic that achieving a more balanced representation of women and minorities in the community college presidency was a realistic goal and one that they are committed to achieve.

VALUING DIVERSITY

The data from this study indicate that to a certain degree more women and minorities are being selected for the community college presidency than in the past. Between 1991 and 1996, the increase for women (7 percentage points) is more than double the increase for minorities (3 percentage points). During this period, 93 female presidents were hired into their current position, and 77 percent of them were new to the presidency.

Although community college governing boards are hiring minority candidates, many of these candidates are moving from one presidency to another. For example, of the 67 minority presidents who were hired into their current position between 1991 and 1996, more than 39 percent moved into their position from another community college presidency. Sixty-one percent of the minorities who were hired into their current position during this five-year period were new to the presidency. In comparison, 72 percent of the Caucasian presidents hired during this same period were new to the presidency. The reason a relatively high percentage of minority presidents move from one presidency to another was not addressed in this research and deserves further study.

The comparison of the percentage of female presidents of public community colleges in 1991 and 1996 indicates that opportunities for women are increasing. During this five-year period, the percentage of female presidents has increased from 11 percent to 18 percent, or approximately one percentage point per year. At that rate, if the goal for female representation is close to 50 percent (to match the female population in the United States), the goal theoretically would be reached in about 32 years—the year 2030.

By calculating the annual increase in percentages for minorities (based upon the increase from 1991 to 1996) and using it to project future hiring, by the year 2030, minorities would constitute 33 percent of the community college presidents. By the year 2030, minorities are expected to make up 50 percent of the United States population.

These calculations address numbers of people and percentages of people, but they do not address the underlying principles encompassed in valuing diversity. The goals of increasing women and minorities in the presidency should not be simply to satisfy numbers or quotas, for quotas serve as ceilings as well as floors for underrepresented groups. The purpose of increasing the percentage of female and minority presidents is to take full benefit of the wealth of their knowledge, skills, and perceptions. Valuing diversity means respecting alternative opinions, alternative approaches, and alternative experiences and including them in the discussion. Valuing diversity means understanding that not everyone experiences the world in the same way and that the richness of these different and differing experiences improves the quality of life for all. In Zelema Harris's words, valuing diversity means "getting over the issue of race or gender" and focusing on the best interests of the institution and the community when selecting a community college president.

6

◆

ESTABLISHING AND MAINTAINING RELATIONSHIPS

Successful presidents establish, maintain, and enhance relationships with selective constituencies of the college for the purpose of promoting the college's well-being. These presidents possess, analyze, improve, and employ the skills and knowledge required to ensure that all of the relationships function in ways that promote the mission and goals of the college.

This description of the role of the successful president assumes that presidents understand which constituencies, out of an almost endless list, require presidential attention at a given point. A list of presidential constituencies might include, for example, the governing board; all segments of the college community, with special emphasis on the faculty; and certain civic, business, political, and educational leaders. Successful presidents understand that although all of the college's constituencies are important, presidents have to establish priorities in working with the college's constituencies, and most of presidents' time and energy must be devoted to working with presidential constituencies.

The above description also assumes that the president knows which skills and knowledge are required to cultivate those relationships that work to promote the college's well-being. Presidents in states with state-level governing boards, in which system chancellors have the major responsibility of working with state legislators, would place working with legislatures lower on their constituency list than would presidents in states with local governing boards and in which the primary responsibility for working with state legislators lies with the presidents. Some presidents' lists will contain constituencies that do not even exist in other states. For example, the president of a college with a bargaining unit would likely rank relations with the union representative high on the constituency list, whereas presidents of colleges without a bargaining unit would have no union constituency.

THE PRESIDENT'S CONSTITUENCY POOL

Leading the nation's community colleges requires not just identifying those skills and abilities required for effective leadership but also determining where, when, and how to employ those skills and abilities (Vaughan, 1994, p. 61). When individuals reach the president's office, they should possess most of the skills and abilities required to be successful presidents. On the other hand, as is true in any profession, these skills and abilities must be constantly enhanced and applied if they are to serve the president and the college to the fullest. For example, in most cases, computer skills are a prerequisite for the successful presidency today. Knowledge and skills associated with the computer had to be learned by many of today's presidents after they assumed the presidency.

Effective presidents need to choose carefully where and how to expend the limited resources of the president's office. Presidents who devote their skills and abilities in the proper arenas will find that their leadership will improve, as will their effectiveness (Vaughan, 1994, p. 78).

No matter at what location or at what point one is president, there are two groups that will always make the president's constituency list: the governing board and the faculty.

If asked whether the president's most important constituency is the governing board or the faculty, many seasoned presidents would answer, "Both of the above." As one scholar observes, "The president is often left teetering between the faculty on the one side and the board on the other. He [or she] is accountable *for* the faculty and *to* the board, but without sufficient wherewithal to satisfy either" (Fisher, 1991, p. 1). Although one may disagree that presidents lack the "wherewithal to satisfy either" the board or the faculty, the fact is that the two groups are the presidents' most important constituencies.

WORKING WITH THE GOVERNING BOARD

Presidents serve at the pleasure of the board, and boards hire presidents. Between the time presidents are employed and the time they leave a given presidency, a relationship exists that plays a major role in determining how well the college functions. The relationship between the board and the president is so important that if the trustee-president team functions well, members of the college community and even the community in general can see the effects of the collaboration; if conflict exists, this too can be sensed (Vaughan & Weisman, 1997, p. 41).

Kerr and Gade (1989), for example, discuss the importance of the president-board relationship in their book on the academic presidency. They write, "A first duty of a board is to assure an effective presidency for the sake of the institution but also for the sake of the board; only with an effective presidency can a board be effective" (Kerr and Gade, 1989, p. 177). In addition to Kerr and Gade, a number of others have written about the president-board relationship, including Carver and Mayhew (1994), Fisher (1991), Kauffman (1980), and Nason (1982).

With the exception of the book by Carver and Mayhew, none of the works deals specifically with the community college. Nevertheless, the common theme found in all of the works is as relevant to community colleges as it is to other institutions of higher education: The president and governing board must work as a team if they are to serve their institutions effectively.

A symbiotic relationship should exist between the board and the president, for a president cannot be effective without an effective board nor can a board be effective without an effective president (PS)[1]. These thoughts come from a president who understands the need to establish the ties that bind the president and board together in ways whereby they "feed upon" each other's work, each growing stronger because of the other's existence. The most lasting and successful relationships are those built upon mutual trust and mutual support.

Mutual Trust

There is a high level of trust between the president and members of the governing board. In a 1995 study of community college trustees and presidents, almost 73 percent of the trustees rated the trust between themselves and their presidents to be very strong; another 21 percent rated it as somewhat strong (CTS). In discussing the need for trust, trustees and presidents alike agreed that honesty, openness, and "no surprises" must be at the basis of trusting relationships (TI; PI). Mutual trust between the president and the board is at the center of their relationship, and it is from this center that many other aspects of the president-board relationship emanate.

---

1. Unless otherwise noted, the trustee information in this chapter is taken from a national study of 618 community college trustees and 299 presidents conducted by the authors in 1995. Data from the trustees' responses are cited as CTS; data from the presidents' responses are cited as PS. Interview responses from 15 trustees are cited as TI and from 10 presidents as PI.

What happens when trust breaks down? The trustees agree that if they do not trust the information given to them by the president, they would share their lack of trust with the board chair and confront the president as a board, not as individuals (TI). Presidents, as is true with trustees, would face the issue of mistrust head on, working primarily through the board chair in an attempt to resolve the issue (PI). If the board has evidence that it cannot trust the president, it has an obligation to deal with the issue efficiently. Presidents who have evidence that they cannot trust the governing board must resolve the issues creating mistrust; otherwise, they have little choice but to move to another position (PI).

Mutual Support

Obviously, if presidents and boards trust each other, they are more likely to support each other than if mistrust exists between the two. In 1995, more than 75 percent of trustees rated the mutual support between themselves and their president to be very strong; another 20 percent rated trust between the president and trustees to be somewhat strong (CTS). Similarly, almost 75 percent of the presidents rated the mutual support between the president and board to be very strong, and another 19 percent rated the mutual support to be somewhat strong (PS).

One trustee offered advice for presidents who wish to maintain the support and trust of the board and for trustees who wish to maintain the support and trust of the president. The trustee asked, "Does the president tell me things I need to know in ways that are very honest and not couching things or putting a slant on them that would be favorable so [the president] can hide things we might not be pleased to hear? I want to know how the president behaves in a crisis situation. Would he or she put his or her interests above the interest of the institution?" (TI).

A president offered similar advice, noting that "the integrity of the president must be constantly maintained, and the board must believe that anything it hears from [the president] must be the truth and nothing but the truth" (PI).

Both presidents and trustees agree that the way to cultivate trust and support is to establish clear lines of communication (TI; PI). Effective communication between the president's office and the board is critical when the college faces a crisis. As one president observes in *New Directions for Community Colleges,*

> An open and harmonious relationship between the president and the board of trustees is essential for effective leadership in the collegiate setting. Although there are many circumstances that can strain this relationship, it is at greatest risk during a crisis, external or internal, predictable or unpredictable. . . . The time to prepare for a crisis is *before* one occurs. With procedures already in place, the timely actions of a president can minimize the impact of a crisis upon the president-board relationship; such actions may even lead to a stronger relationship between them (Fanelli, 1997, pp. 63-64).

Regardless of whether a crisis exists, effective communication between the president and the board is mandatory if the college is to operate well. Trust and support are built upon effective communication.

Providing Information

In 1995, almost 93 percent of the trustees stated that they rely upon presidents and their staffs for most of the information they receive about the college. More than 86 percent of the trustees stated that the president's office exercises the greatest influence on the board's decision (CTS).

In working with the governing board, presidents have an obligation to do their share to create an effective president-board team. The successful team must be built upon trust, mutual support, effective communication, and accurate and adequate information. Successful presidents know that as the college's educational leader and liaison with the board, they must ensure that information is correct, adequate, and communicated effectively to the board. Otherwise, trust and mutual support will be lacking and the president-board team will not function in ways that promote to the fullest extent possible the well-being of the college.

THE PRESIDENT AND FACULTY

Unfortunately, much of the literature on community college presidential leadership spends scant time explaining the relationship between the president and the faculty. Yet presidents who ignore this relationship or take it for granted do so at their peril. As Robert Birnbaum notes, "The faculty represent the institution's academic programs and its commitment to academic values. Faculty are obligated to judge whether the missions of the creation and dissemination of knowledge are being honored, whether a president is appropriately concerned with curriculum and student development, . . . and whether the president operates in a manner consistent with a collegial community" (1992, p. 58). Further, Birnbaum believes, "faculty support of a president over the long run may strengthen positive attributions of leadership and enhance the president's ability to influence the interpretations of others" (p. 168). Faculty support, Birnbaum contends, is at least as important as board support.

The subject of president-faculty relations is important in placing presidential constituencies in proper perspective. The board makes policy and the president implements policy. Communication between the faculty and the governing board takes place through the president. A major challenge for presidents and trustees is to establish and employ avenues through which the faculty can communicate with board members without leaving the president out of the loop.

Communication

How do presidents perceive communication between the faculty and the board taking place? Seventy-one percent of the presidents responding to the 1995 survey stated that communication between the faculty and the board takes place either through the president (43 percent) or with the president's knowledge (28 percent). On the other hand, 29 percent of the presidents (almost double the percentage of trustees) perceive that faculty communicate with the board without the president's knowledge (PS).

More than 1 out of every 7 trustees (15.4 percent) perceive that faculty members communicate with the board without the president's involvement or knowledge (CTS). Close to 1 out of 3 presidents (29 percent) perceive that faculty communicate with the board without the presidents' knowledge (PS). The discrepancy is probably a matter of perception.

What is the true picture regarding the president's role in faculty communications with the board? Based on the responses of both presidents and trustees, the conclusion is that in the great majority of the cases, communication between the faculty and the board occurs with the president's involvement or knowledge. The answer is less clear regarding the proportion of faculty who communicate with the board without the president's involvement or knowledge, for the perceptions of presidents and trustees vary widely on the subject.

If the governing board has a policy that dictates that communication between the faculty and board takes place only through the president, the perception of trustees is likely to be that the policy is being followed; otherwise trustees would be at fault for not following their own policy. Moreover, if trustees discuss faculty concerns without the president's involvement or knowledge, it may be that the president perceives that the faculty members, as opposed to the trustees, have bypassed the president's office. For the most part, trustees probably adhere to the policy regarding faculty communication with the board. And as long as no major problems occur as a result of faculty bypassing the president when communicating with the board, both presidents and trustees are probably willing to "let it slide." Nevertheless, it is good practice and good policy for all communication that influences the operation of the college to flow from the faculty through the president to the board.

To bypass the president in the communication process is to court a potential building of mistrust and a loss of support between the president and the board. All presidents should examine how faculty communicate with the board and share their findings with the board (Vaughan & Weisman, 1997). If there is no policy on faculty-board communication that includes the president in all steps of the process, one should be developed. If there is a policy and faculty are ignoring it, then the policy should be enforced, with all leaks from the faculty to the board patched. It is important, though, that presidents not "take on the faculty" on what is rightly a board policy question. Rather, presidents should take their concerns regarding communication between the faculty and board to the board chairs; the board should then take action, either developing new policy or enforcing existing policy. *The president must not be placed in the middle of any disagreement over how the faculty communicate with the board.* For presidents to end up in the middle of a policy disagreement between the faculty and the board is to risk losing the support of one or both groups. No president can afford to alienate even one of his or her most important constituencies, much less both.

Policy

One president interviewed commented that presidents must be sensitive to faculty when making changes. Faculty members who have been with the college for a number of years might feel uncomfortable with change, according to this president. She stated that it is the president's responsibility to make faculty members feel comfortable with change and to see that the changes are both orderly and adequately funded (PI).

Two of the presidents interviewed in 1995, while not relating faculty tenure to change, nevertheless noted that faculty do not always endorse changes, especially changes in the college's mission. One president noted that faculty members in degree programs (both technical and transfer) at the college where he is president feel that noncredit offerings are threatening the core offerings of the college by drawing students away from credit courses. The same president noted that he and the faculty are working together to ensure that developmental education remains a part of the mission, including seeing that it is placed in its proper perspective in relation to the remainder of the college's mission (PI).

Similarly, the second president noted that when resources are scarce, faculty members want to return to the core of the mission which they, the faculty, define as transfer and upper-end technical programs (PI). Developmental education has also come under attack by the faculty, who want students who are better prepared academically and more motivated to achieve a college education.

In both of the above situations, the president has the major responsibility for ensuring that the chasm between faculty and the president's office does not become too wide to bridge. Presidents must explain why change is taking place, what impact it will have on the college's mission and on its faculty, and how it will be funded. Faculty, on the other hand, must realize that no community college today can, as one president noted, "resemble what it was in the 1960s" (PI).

Another president interviewed identified a major challenge for presidents and faculty in their joining together to take charge of their own destiny. Taking charge, to this president at least, means being accountable to the board and the public for improving productivity and educational outcomes. He and his administrative team work closely with the union to assure the college's governing board and representatives of state government that the faculty and administration are bringing about needed changes in the college's operation, eliminating any need for the members of the board or state leaders to intrude into the daily operations of the college (PI).

CLOSING THE LOOP

In considering their two most important constituencies, successful community college presidents are aware of the following:

- Presidents, trustees, and faculty members need to understand they all have a high stake in the college's success. To one degree or another, they are legally, professionally, ethically, and personally responsible for the success of the college.

- By working together, the president and board can expand their symbiotic relationship to include the faculty. Once the three elements come together as one unit with one goal—promoting the college's welfare— a situation results whereby what is good for the college is good for the president, the board, and the faculty. They form a loop, reinforcing with each turn the concept that what is good for the college is good for all concerned.

∎ Presidents and their two most important constituencies
should work together to see that all of the college's other
constituencies are served effectively.

The definition of the role of a successful community college
president could be broadened to define the successful college: A
successful college is one in which the president, trustees, and
faculty members cultivate relationships with the college's constituencies for the purpose of promoting the college's well-being.
Members of these groups possess, analyze, improve, and employ
the skills and knowledge required to ensure that all of the relationships they establish with the college's constituencies function
in ways that promote the mission and goals of the college.

If presidents can bring their two most important constituencies into an alliance in which all members promote the mission
and goals of the college, they have established relationships that
will ensure their own success and the success of the college.

7

---◆---

ISSUES FACING COMMUNITY
COLLEGE LEADERS AT THE
MILLENNIUM

The last two questions on the presidential survey asked the
presidents to identify the major issues facing the community college within the next four or five years and what they,
as presidents, can do to prepare their colleges to face the
issues. This chapter presents information gained from the surveys, followed by responses to interview questions regarding
the skills and traits that will be required of a president in the
21st century.

IDENTIFYING THE ISSUES

The consistency with which the issues showed up on survey
after survey illustrates what presidents nationwide perceive to
be the critical issues facing community colleges in the near
future. Many of the issues overlap. Presidents who listed funding as an issue have only one legitimate use for funds: to
accomplish the college's mission. Presidents who listed technology as an issue in the teaching and learning process would have
to consider funding and mission in dealing with the issue of
technology.

Funding. Although not all of the presidents responding to the survey listed funding as the most critical issue facing the community college within the next few years, funding was listed by more presidents than any other issue. More than one-half of the presidents perceived a lack of adequate funding as the most critical issue.

One president noted that a major issue facing the community college is maintaining open access and quality in the face of significant financial constraints. This president placed the college's mission at the heart of the debate on funding. Another president stated that community colleges are expected to deal with a dramatic increase in enrollments at a time when the resources provided by the state are declining. From another president came the following: "Funding continues to be the biggest hurdle to performing our mission." Similarly, another president noted that "funding will continue to be a major issue, especially as the number of high school graduates increases." In another's words, "There will be less money coupled with more demands for accountability and outcomes assessment and services."

Issues surrounding funding go to the very heart of American society and the community college's role in society. One president painted a picture of "a growing class system in America with the haves–have-nots, the employed–unemployed, and a growing middle class with low ceilings. The rapid growth of technology is passing the have-nots by, many of whom will never be able to catch up, and they will quit trying." Another president stated that the "public will increase its resistance to unlimited facility growth for established institutions. Thus many structures such as semesters, weekly meeting of classes, and on-campus instruction will be altered. There will be an increased reluctance by the public to provide financial support for these structures." Noting changes at the federal level, another president asserted that "the major issue facing community colleges is the decreased level of funding and the increased need for services. This will become more apparent with welfare reform."

As one president expressed it, "The major issue facing community colleges in the next three to four years will be how to address all of the issues that the local community leaders, state leaders and legislators, and federal leaders have discovered that this uniquely American institution can effectively address, if given the funding to do so."

Technology. According to the survey responses, the next most critical issue facing the community college within the coming three or four years is the role of technology in the educational process. As is true with funding, issues associated with technology cut across most colleges' activities. The key concerns regarding technology seem to be its cost; its use in teaching and learning; its use in support services such as admissions, registration, and record keeping, and in the college's financial operation; its use in workforce development; and its quick obsolescence, which places a burden on the college to keep it current. The concerns regarding technology could be summarized by what we need, how we pay for it, and what we do with it.

In one president's words, "The impact of telecommunications will be the major issue facing the community college in the next three or four years, accompanied by pressures to abandon elements of the college's mission. There will be a vast array of educational choices offered electronically, and we will be tempted either to chase them all or ignore them all. The challenge will be to find the right balance of activity appropriate to our mission."

After technology, the number of presidents identifying a single issue as the most significant one decreased considerably, although in many cases these other issues incorporated the need for resources or technology or both as a way of defining the issue and seeking a solution. The following were mentioned as critical issues facing the community college in the next four or five years: leadership and governance; workforce training and working with business and industry; responding to change, including organizational restructuring; and accountability and mission. These issues are discussed below.

Leadership and Governance. What is needed in the future, according to one president, is "effective, knowledgeable, honest leaders who have the ability to motivate others and lead by example." One president identified as the most critical issue the development of a system of governance that includes the faculty and staff as partners with the president and board in the decision-making process. One president called for "an environment that nurtures and values stability and continuity for leaders." Another president feared that trustees will become involved in the everyday management of the college, causing "the line between policy and administration to become blurred." Similarly, one president remained "in a regents system because I do not want to work for a local board." One president noted that the most critical issue facing the community college "is providing confident leaders and solid academic experiences in a climate that does not provide steady economic and social support." The issue of providing adequate leadership for the community college could be considered the umbrella under which the following issues reside. Yet there is understanding to be gained by examining the other issues apart from leadership.

Interacting with Change. The successful community college, according to one president, must "establish a culture that welcomes change as an opportunity and must have a commitment to deal with the challenges of an uncertain and ambiguous future while maintaining quality and accountability." Crossing several issue boundaries, a president noted that "the major issue facing the community college is change. Community colleges are going to have to adapt to new technologies, to sharing resources, and to collaborative partnerships."

Sounding less than optimistic, one president listed the most critical issue for community colleges as "being relevant to the changing educational needs in a changed society. I wonder at times if many of us presidents are in a 'last hurrah'; or, I wonder, are we truly on the edge of a new relevance and new growth. It can go either way for us. Many community colleges may be totally marginalized."

According to one president, to be successful, community colleges must "understand the needs of an interdependent world. Curricular needs demand change—the new world order changes the way we must teach, what we must learn, and how we fund education." Similarly, another president stated that "just as corporations have been forced in the recent past to rethink the way they do business, community colleges too will be required to make several fundamental changes to address an entirely new set of student needs." Another comment illustrates that many subissues extend from larger issues:

> In my view, the major issue facing the community college in the next three to four years—and probably beyond—is to find ways to respond creatively and imaginatively to the massive, sweeping, and fast-paced changes taking place in so many areas and coming from so many directions. Many changes are related to technology; others are more directly related to demographics, staffing, mission, and the delivery of education.

Workforce Development. Worker preparation has been a focus of community colleges for at least half a century. In the 1980s, working with business and industry became a prerequisite for successful community colleges. Although workforce development may have become institutionalized at many colleges, thereby not appearing to have the same intensity today as an issue that it had in the late 1980s and early 1990s, a number of

presidents responding to the survey placed workforce development at the top of their list of critical issues. One president
noted that "the national response to business and industry and
to short-term or noncredit job training" is the major issue.
Another president stated that "increasing and cementing the
role of community colleges in career and job skills education
and in economic development at the local, state, and national
levels is the major issue facing community colleges."

In a similar vein, a president asserted that the issue facing
the community college in the near future is "becoming learning
colleges that focus the mission on meeting the economic development needs of your community, the expanding high school
population, and business and industry." From another president came the following: "The major issue is adjusting to new
workforce development legislation that will require either dras-
tic downsizing or providing more individualized short-term
training programs." Another president cited "preparing the
increasing number of students whom we are likely to enroll at
the community college for the workplace in the 21st century
and upgrading the current workforce to meet the increased
technological needs of business and industry" as the most critical issues facing the community college. According to one survey respondent,

> Community college leaders need to study the profile of stu-
> dents attending or who are eligible to attend their institutions
> and the requirements of the business and industries in the com-
> munity. Armed with this knowledge, the curriculum, schedul-
> ing, and other activities of the college should fit that profile.
> Current practice is too often based on faculty competencies
> and contracts that lock a college into courses for which there
> is limited demand by students or the businesses and industries
> in the community.

Whether community colleges will be so successful in preparing workers in the years ahead that workforce development will

no longer be an issue remains to be seen. For now, it seems highly likely that workforce training will remain a critical issue for some colleges well into the next century.

Accountability and Mission. Holding presidents accountable for what the community college accomplishes, like many of the issues identified by current presidents, has been a concern of legislators and the general public for several decades. Indeed, the accountability bandwagon seems to make frequent stops on the community campus, as it should if the colleges are to fulfill their roles as the people's college. Accountability for what? For fulfilling the college's mission in a responsible way. A number of presidents identified accountability and understanding the mission as the major issues facing the community college in the next few years. Their responses provide some new perspectives and insights into the importance of the issues. One president suggested that the major issue is "being able to explain adequately our importance to the public and maybe just as important, being able to agree collectively as community college leaders why we are such an important institution." Another president stated that "legitimizing our role and mission in light of increasing attacks on public education" is a major issue. Similarly, another president noted that "the major issue is demonstrating our effectiveness so that the public has confidence in our administrators. Once the confidence level is raised, there should be less anxiety." Another president got down to the basics: "The major issue is accountability—proving to our local boards, local, state, and national governments, and to our citizens that we are using funds and resources wisely and that learning is happening."

Comments on the mission by current presidents, while varied, are enlightening. One president feared "the erosion of the transfer function"; another one wanted "to restructure our mission to help communities better address critical issues." One president noted that with "less funding for all social needs, I see community colleges needing to defend their missions strongly," otherwise other agencies and educational entities will want a part of the community college's mission in order "to justify their own funding." In a similar vein, another president observed that "how we respond to external forces impacting our mission will have a major determination on our future and funding sources." Another president observed that community colleges "may be taking themselves out of higher education to become training institutions; national leadership may be leading in the wrong direction for long-term values and the mission." (The president did not identify the national leadership referred to in the above statement.)

Interpreting the mission of the community college to the college's various constituents is critical if these colleges are to receive adequate support. The preceding quotes illustrate how complex the mission is to interpret and why it is important that community college presidents have a clear vision of the role of the community college as the nation moves toward the year 2000.

A Potpourri of Issues. The remaining issues identified by those presidents responding to the survey cover a number of topics. Although funding and technology received the most attention, other issues that came up included dealing with students who are academically unprepared for college, maintaining enrollments at a level commensurate with the college mission, and retirement and retraining of senior faculty.

Maintaining enrollments emerged as a double-edged issue. Some presidents feared "flat" or declining enrollments; others (as discussed earlier) worried about being able to handle, without additional resources, what they perceive as the oncoming flood of students. One president's comments on enrollments placed the debate in perspective: "Enrollment is a major challenge because of the impact it has on other items." Any president who has ever struggled with a budget understands and appreciates this president's observation, for enrollments often drive the budget, which in turn drives much of what the college does.

One president summed it up this way: The challenge is to "provide leadership in changing community colleges so that they can properly utilize information and other communications technologies; maintain accessible and affordable educational opportunities; respond satisfactorily to public expectations for documented accountability; serve effectively the growing number of culturally diverse students; and understand the increasing interdependence of our world."

RESPONDING TO THE ISSUES

In addition to identifying the issues, the presidents were asked to provide their perspective on preparing their colleges to respond to the issues. The following responses represent the views of a number of presidents.

Regarding the issue of inadequate funding, the responses overwhelmingly centered on obtaining funds from private sources. Resource development showed up often in the responses. A number of presidents suggested that they must see that their colleges become more efficient in using existing and future resources.

Although presidents of the future will seek additional sources of revenue, a major source of funds for most community colleges will continue to be state and local tax dollars. A large number of presidents commented that to prepare the community college for the future, presidents must work more often and more effectively with state legislators and local political leaders.

In facing issues revolving around technology, the presidents' responses were quite varied. The following comments capture many of the concerns a number of presidents have regarding technology and the community college's future. One president's solution is to "gradually change priorities to cause technology to be viewed as a continuous required expenditure." Another president stated that presidents must "try to build an institutional awareness regarding the advantages of technologies and to try to calm the paranoia and apprehensiveness of faculty and staff regarding possible negative effects technological advances have on enrollment, programs, tenure, and so on." Another president would prepare the college this way: "make administrative and instructional technology a priority in meeting the college's mission; develop a technology plan for the institution; develop a technology task force to oversee equipment and software standardization and purchasing, equipment replacement, inventory and cross usage of equipment, and software across campus; and recommend faculty training." (A number of presidents proposed the development of such a plan.)

Developing leadership for a community college that will sustain it in the future is a complex and comprehensive undertaking. In general, the presidents who offered their perceptions on preparing the college for the future would lead by example. One president's remarks on leadership present this perspective: "As president, I must encourage, model, expect, and support learning and risk taking. Through my words, actions, decisions, and relationships I must communicate my faith in our collective ability to shape our organization to respond to and function effectively in a future that will be very different from all of our pasts."

If the mission is not understood, it is the president's role to articulate the mission more clearly. As one president noted, "We must inform the public about our mission and funding problems and prove that we are doing a good job." One way of promoting understanding and support for the mission, according to a number of presidents, is to build partnerships with other community agencies and organizations. The partnership will help in obtaining funds, promoting the mission, and in keeping programs and courses current.

Accomplishing much of the above and preparing to face the issues in the future requires planning according to a number of presidents. As one president said, "We must plan, plan, plan." Another president commented that to be successful in the future, presidents "must understand what will impact the college over the next decade, identify a response strategy, move to implement a plan to achieve the strategic objectives, and work like blazes with as broad a base of colleagues as possible to achieve success."

LEADERSHIP FOR THE NEXT CENTURY

Tomorrow's community college presidents will resemble today's presidents and the presidents of five years ago in terms of career paths, educational background, and in various other ways. For example, it is likely that the most traveled pathway to the presidency will continue to be the academic pipeline, since more than 50 percent of the current presidents served as their college's chief academic officer before assuming their first presidency. Most presidencies of the future will probably be filled by those who have a doctorate, which is likely to be in higher education. The president of the future will probably come from within the community college ranks, as did more than 90 percent of today's presidents.

Community college presidents in the future will have many of the same experiences that yesterday's and today's presidents have had. Tomorrow's presidents will work with, be influenced by, and, in many cases, be mentored by current presidents. Since trustees will continue to turn to current presidents for recommendations and advice as they choose future presidents, current presidents will help shape the views and actions of today's governing boards regarding tomorrow's presidents.

In addition to having similar experiences and educational backgrounds, most community college presidents of the future will function much as today's presidents function, because they will move into campus cultures that have been established over decades. In most cases, to be successful or even survive in the presidency, incoming presidents, whether entering the presidency today or 10 years from now, must rely upon the support systems inherent in the college's culture.

On the other hand, the "face" of the presidency is changing. The percentage of female community college presidents has increased by 7 percentage points over the past five years. Women are in the presidential pipeline, in academics and other areas. A large number of women are in doctoral programs in higher education, the degree of choice for current community college presidents. Although men will probably dominate the presidency in the immediate future, it is clear that women are now major players and will continue to increase both in numbers and influence in the future.

The news has been less encouraging for minorities. Over the last five years, the percentage of minority presidents has increased from approximately 11 percent to approximately 14 percent. One solution to placing more minorities in the presidency is to get more minority applicants into the presidential pipeline. Mentoring must begin early in their careers. A good starting point would be the time when minorities enter the community college. If every community college president would agree to serve as a mentor to one student member of a minority group for a two-year period—working with a different community college student at the end of the two years—a start could be made to filling the pipeline to the presidency. The mentoring process would include introducing the student to higher education leadership as a profession, with special emphasis on the role of the president. Presidents, many of whom are fond of holding leadership seminars for students, could discuss the community college presidency as a career option. Law, medicine, engineering, and many of the academic disciplines recruit students at the beginning of their college careers, which should be the case with higher education leadership.

Current presidents should expand professional opportunities for women and minorities who wish to move into the presidency. These professional experiences include providing women and minorities with the opportunity to earn a doctorate and serving as mentors for those women and minorities who want to become presidents. Boards of trustees should make every effort to include women and minorities in the pool of applicants when seeking to fill a presidency. For the percentage of female and minority presidents to increase, current trustees and presidents must assist, encourage, and help orchestrate the move into the presidency.

PREPARING FOR THE PRESIDENCY

The presidents interviewed were presented with the following scenario and asked to provide their comments. (See chapter 4 for a list of the presidents interviewed.)

Q: Nearly 45 percent of the presidents stated that they plan to retire within the next six years. Imagine that you were contacted by the governing board of a community college in another state for assistance in developing its selection criteria for a new president. What skills and traits do you feel will be the most important ones for the community college president in the 21st century?

Boggs pointed out that he has been president at his institution for 12 years:

The skills I need today are different from the skills that I needed when I first came into the job. I expect they are going to be different in the future. I think one thing that is and will continue to be important is the ability to involve other people successfully in the governance of the college. When the college was first founded, it required a very strong, somewhat autocratic, kind of leader to get the job done quickly. We are now finding that we have to involve both faculty and staff and sometimes even students through shared governance. We are going to need leaders who are able to do that, still get the job done, and still focus on the long-term needs of the college. I think that is an important skill.

Fund-raising is certainly something that I never had training in, and it wasn't important when I first came to Palomar, but it has become very important. I think presidents in the future will need to know about technology, for technology is going to be important. Of course, legislative advocacy skills are going to continue to be important. We are going to need to be advocates for our colleges with Congress and the state legislature. Community skills are important. We've got to be out there in the community, and that's not going to diminish in the future.

Dassance answered the question regarding the skills and traits presidents will require in the 21st century as follows: "I think the most important characteristic would have to be along the lines of participatory management. I believe that the organizations that are going to be successful are those that use the talents and resources of everybody in the organization." According to Dassance, to move the institution into participatory management "requires very good interpersonal skills. I think it probably requires being able to get beyond ego. I think the future is going to require someone who can live with a great deal of ambiguity, who has good political skills, negotiating skills, conflict resolution skills, who is development oriented in the sense of understanding that a part of the role of the president is to be a part of the institutional development effort." He suggested that presidents will need to "look at every opportunity as a development opportunity, whether it's private fundraising, grants, coalitions, or whatever. In some ways, the president of the future will have to be more like a mayor than we past and current presidents have been."

Giles's successful leader at the millennium will be someone who is "a consensus builder, a participatory manager, and one who values and supports collaboration. The successful leader will be a president who, even though he or she may not have a full understanding of technology and how it works, recognizes the absolute necessity of incorporating technology into everything that we are doing in the community college, both on the administrative and instructional side. The successful leader is also a user of technology in terms of computers, e-mail and so on." To be successful, Giles asserted that the president "should be outgoing, civic minded, and willing to get involved in the community and with community agencies." Giles realizes that future presidents cannot exist on some self-created island." I guess the last thing is that the president must be willing to be challenged in his or her thinking by the people with whom he or she is working, which brings the discussion back to consensus builder, participatory manager, and not an autocrat."

Harris believes that successful presidents in the next century "have to be good communicators, and they have to love people and really believe in the goodness of people, because that is the only way you are going to bring about the kind of change that is going to be needed in our organizations in the next six or so years." Building upon her concern for people, Harris stated that this love must manifest itself through "a strong commitment to learners. Presidents have got to know and believe that the community college can provide the best possible programs and services for people coming to us. Presidents have got to have some understanding of what goes on in the classroom and how people learn. That's the only way you are going to be able to inform the faculty or hire the right person to influence faculty." Harris believes that educating the board is a role the future president must fill. She noted, "Presidents have to feel comfortable in their role of educating the board. I believe my major role in this regard is to influence the board and to educate the members on what my role is and what their role is." Like some of the other presidents interviewed, Harris feels that presidents in the future "have to be comfortable getting out there raising money and meeting with legislators." Finally, she believes that "presidents of the future must be visionaries and have some knowledge of the whole technological revolution and an understanding of how it is going to affect their college."

Ku offered a succinct summary of which skills and attributes he feels the successful president will need in the next century. "There are three skills: leadership skills, financial management and fund-raising skills, and skills in understanding inside and out the whole college's operation and working with the faculty to make sure they are with us and not moving in a different direction." He noted that working with the faculty "is critical and takes some experience and skill. Not just anybody can do it."

Myran believes that "the most important thing is that presidents be persons who passionately care about the community college's mission and demonstrate through their own behavior that they can be extremely creative and successful in achieving that mission." Myran also believes that "future presidents are going to have to demonstrate that they are tuned in to some of the trends in organizational development, such as being oriented toward teamwork rather than individual performance and having some capacity to bring about cultural change, so that they are creating a more participatory, more team-based environment on campus." Myran made an interesting observation that contradicts those individuals who see the external demands on the presidency increasing. He described "a trend where presidents again are expected to be educational leaders, to be able to work with the faculty, to be able to make curriculum and teaching the center of organizational life, perhaps a movement back inside the college in terms of shaping those central resources—the faculty, the curriculum—in balance with community and state activities."

Perkins, while noting that many of the skills and traits that served community college presidents so well in the 1960s, 1970s, and 1980s are still required today and will be required in the future, offered his views of the skills that will be required in the future that may not have been as important in the past three decades:

> I think that being able to work with groups in a team environment will be important. The kind of leader who was sort of autocratic or dictatorial and who could have been successful in the past will have a very difficult time in the future, if not now. I see more of a team player, a president who can mediate and negotiate and work with groups is required now and will be in the future. Second, the successful president in the future will be an individual who is sensitive, who is committed to working with different populations, who understands issues of diversity, and who is sensitive to the issues and is willing to bring people together. Third, the president of the future needs to have a good, solid, conceptual understanding of some of the basic skills related to technology. I think presidents need to be aware of the limitations and opportunities of technology. Next, I've found that a greater understanding of finances is important. I find myself, unfortunately, spending more time on finances than I do on curriculum. Finally, I would say the last skill required is being able to forge a partnership with other agencies so that not only does it benefit the community college, but it has the benefit of helping those other organizations do their job also.

Perkins offered a warning regarding technology. He finds more and more people "looking at technology as a solution to problems and not understanding that the technology itself is going to be creating problems. It's almost as if people believe that if we just buy more computers and hook us all up, then everything will be better." He noted that presidents in the future are going to have to understand "what issues are going to have to be resolved as a result of putting in technology."

Sanchez believes the following about the successful president in the future:

> The president must envision what is happening in society in general and particularly in the world of work. The community college president must exhibit leadership capabilities of being able to work with constituencies outside the institution and within the institution, like the governing board and other entities within the campus community. The leader must know when to delegate and when to personally take charge of things. The successful president must be able to live with a lot of ambiguity. The president must be an individual who is not afraid to take some risks.

Spina shared his perspective of the presidency based upon his long tenure in the position:

> Tomorrow's presidents need to be better listeners than my generation of presidents. We were brought up in different times, and I think many of us were people of action and sometimes we did something and then went back to the faculty or trustees and told them what we did. I think we have to listen better. We are stressing out some of our stakeholders, especially our faculty. They are teaching more students, they're under the gun, and their accountability levels are higher. So I think we need to pay much more attention to thoughtful approaches with them, to hear what they have to say, and to do a fair amount of consulting. I think that's what new presidents are going to have to do.

In addition to being better listeners, Spina believes that "one of the underestimated attributes for success for college presidents today and tomorrow is physical and emotional stamina." He believes that understanding "the physical and emotional toll of the presidency is a criteria for success. A lot of us are type A personalities, and people feel that we can just sort of go on forever. But I see limitations in myself now. I've gotten off some boards because I can't devote quality time to them."

Spina's final comments concern the need for future presidents to be willing and able to make decisions. "The last important criterion for tomorrow's leadership is making decisions without looking back. There is a lot of postponing of decisions under the justification that all decisions need to be data driven." If the data are available, use them, Spina advised. But he noted that "presidents just have to make some decisions, and I see a lot of my colleagues, frankly, just procrastinating. If you are going to be a president and accept the big bucks we make, you should be able to make some decisions."

Thor summarized her views of presidents of the future: "I think it is important that they have a sense of humor, be able to handle a great deal of stress and pressure, and that they have a vision and passion for where the community college can be in the future." Thor thinks it is important that presidents "be able to build consensus around that vision and create in their college communities enthusiasm for the vision. They also have to be able to deal creatively with declining resources and pressure from special interest groups." Thor believes that the future presidents might follow a different pipeline than those of the past. She noted, "I think some of the things that we have traditionally looked for, such as strong academic backgrounds, are less important now than the ability to create consensus with very diverse groups and create what I call a shared vision of where the institution needs to go."

Thornley looks to the inner self for her president of the future. "The everlasting characteristic to look for is a character-based, principle-centered human being because we need somebody who can be a leader and a servant." She believes also that negotiation skills are mandatory, for "what we as college presidents do winds up under the rubric of negotiations whether you are dealing with the faculty, your employees, your students, the state legislature, community groups, or whether you're raising money, or explaining your county budget."

Wallace stated that "there are six characteristics that I would look for in a 21st century community college president: a learning-centered philosophy; currency with regard to technology; a very strong outcomes and performance orientation to leadership and the evaluation of institutional effectiveness; a commitment to responsiveness; strong support of innovation; and a strong belief in collaboration, both internally and externally."

Wallin believes that the 21st century president will "have to be, first and foremost, a consensus builder and will have to have a high tolerance for ambiguity. The president will have to be externally oriented and have absolutely boundless, limitless energy and time, because the commitments of the position are probably much more than anyone coming from the outside thinks." Sensitive to changing demographics, she believes that the president of the future "needs to be very skilled in dealing with a multicultural setting, dealing with minorities whose enrollments are increasing rapidly in many sectors of our community colleges, and being sensitive to minority needs and issues."

Based on the interviews, the following are prerequisites for a successful presidency in the year 2000 and beyond:

- The president of the future must bring all segments of the college community into the governing process. Shared governance will replace autocratic presidents, where they still exist, and will replace at least some of the bureaucracy associated with community college governance.

- If shared governance is to be effective, the successful president of the future will have to lead the way in reaching consensus on the issues facing the community college and on defining and implementing resolutions to issues. To build consensus, the president will have to be a successful mediator.

- The successful president will have to have a good understanding of the role technology can and should play in the community college's future. Understanding technology implies that the president understands the cost, use, and problems associated with technology.

- Perhaps even more so than in the past, the successful president of the future will have to have a high tolerance for ambiguity.

- The successful president of the future will understand and appreciate multiculturalism with its many manifestations and will use that understanding and appreciation to ensure that the community college serves all segments of society equally and well.

- The successful president of the future will play a major role in building coalitions with other community agencies and organizations. These coalitions will be used in program development, obtaining resources, and in other ways that help the college fulfill its mission.

An issue alluded to in the interviews that presidents must deal with in the future is how to balance internal and external duties and responsibilities. The president of the future must decide how much time and energy to devote to external constituencies and how much time and energy to devote to members of the college community. Is the president to become a "super fund-raiser" who builds coalitions yet neglects the educational process? If so, the question might well become, "Raise funds and build coalitions for what?" On the other hand, can the president ever "go home again" and devote much of the day to making curricular decisions, working with the faculty on a one-on-one basis, and in general assume a position of prominence in the teaching and learning process? Each president will have to strike the proper balance between external and internal demands at each unique institution.

There will never be a magic formula for leading the nation's 1,000 or so public community colleges. Founding presidents, with vision and energy, established a community college institution that has endured and evolved. Today's presidents have had to bridge the past to the present, building on the experiences of the founding presidents. In the years ahead, community college presidents will continue to lead, meeting the challenges and changes of a new century and a new millennium. It is hoped that by understanding the nature of the community college presidency, those serving in this role will be better prepared to lead their colleges in the future.

APPENDIX I
SURVEY INSTRUMENT

This questionnaire will take only about 15 minutes to complete. Please complete and return it in the enclosed self-addressed envelope to George B. Vaughan, Department of Adult and Community College Education, North Carolina State University, Box 7801, Raleigh, NC 27695-7801. If you have any questions, contact Dr. Vaughan at 919-515-6294. **ALL RESPONSES WILL BE KEPT CONFIDENTIAL.**

I. PROFESSIONAL BACKGROUND

1. State: _____

2. Number of years in your present position: _____

3. Did you move into your current position from another community college presidency?   (1) Yes   (2) No

4. Total number of years that you have been a community college president: _____

5. Including your current presidency, how many community college presidencies have you held? _____

6. How old were you when you assumed your first presidency? _____

7. Position held prior to your first presidency:
   (1) Chief Academic Officer   (2) Chief Student Services Officer (3) Chief Business Officer
   (4) V.P. <u>with</u> Academic Overview   (5) V.P. <u>without</u> Academic Overview
   (6) Dean of Community Svcs/Continuing Ed.   (7) Other: _____

8. Were you an internal candidate at the college at which you assumed your first presidency?   (1) Yes   (2) No

9. Was your first presidency in the state in which you finished high school?   (1) Yes   (2) No

II. PROFESSIONAL ACTIVITIES AND PERCEPTIONS

10. How many hours each week do you spend performing the duties associated with the president's office? _____

11. Have you taught in a community college?   (1) Yes, Full-time   (2) Yes, Part-time   (3) No

12. Do you currently teach a course at your community college at least once a year?   (1) Yes   (2) No

13. To which of the following professional organizations do you belong?
    (1) AAHE   (2) AAUW   (3) AERA   (4) APCA   (5) ASHE   (6) NACUBO
    (7) NASPA   (8) NAWE   (9) PDK   (10) Other discipline-based professional organization

14. While president, have you ever submitted a manuscript for publication?
    (1) Yes (Answer questions 14a and 14b.)   (2) No (Skip to question 15.)

    14a. What type of manuscript did you submit? (Please circle all that apply.)
         (1) Opinion article for a newspaper   Was it published?   (1) Yes (2) No
         (2) Article for a professional/trade journal   Was it published?   (1) Yes (2) No
         (3) Book review for a professional/trade journal Was it published? (1) Yes (2) No
         (4) Chapter for a book   Was it published?   (1) Yes (2) No
         (5) Book/monograph manuscript   Was it published?   (1) Yes (2) No
         (6) I have written something other than items listed above for publication.
         Specify: _____   Was it published?   (1) Yes (2) No

    14b. Of the writing you have done, what would you say was the topic of most value to other community college presidents?_____

15. In your role as community college president, on which of the following subjects do you seek information through journals, books or other publications? (Please circle all that apply.)
    (1) Community college issues   (2) Higher education (all sectors) issues   (3) Government/political issues
    (4) Economic issues   (5) Business/private sector issues   (6) Technological issues
    (7) Models of good institutional practice
    (8) Other: _____

16. On a scale from 1 to 3, please rate how useful your knowledge of the following subjects is to you in your role as community college president. (1 = very useful, 2 = useful, 3 = not very useful) Please rate all subject areas.

_____Community college curriculum   _____Community college leadership
_____Collaboration with other public agencies   _____Collaboration with the private sector
_____Community college mission   _____Community college facilities
_____Community college students   _____Community college teaching
_____Community college funding/budget   _____Community college trustees
_____Community college human resources/personnel   _____Other:_____

17. Which two community college/higher education journals or newspapers provide the most valuable information to you as a community college president?_____

18. How likely are you to seek or accept another full-time position within the next five years?
(1) Very likely (Answer question 18a.)
(2) Somewhat likely (Answer question 18a.)
(3) Not likely (Skip to question 19.)

     18a. If you are likely to seek or accept another full-time position within the next five years, into what kind of position do you plan to move?

         (1) Another community college presidency   (2) Four-year college presidency
         (3) Chancellor of a state community college system   (4) Community college faculty
         (5) Political office   (6) Government position
         (7) Business, industry, or private sector position   (8) University professor
         (9) Educational consultant   (10) Other:_____

19. When do you plan to retire from the presidency?:
(1) 1-3 years   (2) 4-6 years   (3) 7-10 years   (4) 10 or more years

20. At what age do you plan to retire? _____

21. Who is your chief confidante; that is, if you have a major problem associated with your role as president, in whom do you confide most often? (Please use the person's title, not his or her name.)
On campus: _____   Off campus: _____

22. At what level of risk do you consider the community college presidency to be?
(1) High risk   (2) Moderate risk   (3) Low risk

23. How stressful do you consider the community college presidency to be?
(1) High stress   (2) Moderate stress   (3) Low stress

III. EMPLOYMENT INFORMATION

24. Is your employment contract
(1) Fixed   (2) Rolling contract   (3) Other: _____

25. For how many years is your contract? _____

26. Do you live in a college-owned house?   (1) Yes (Skip to question 27.)   (2) No (Answer question 26a.)

     26a. If no, do you receive a housing allowance? (1) Yes (Answer question 26b.)   (2) No

     26b. If yes, amount of monthly allowance _____

27. How many days of annual leave (vacation time) do you earn each year? _____

28. How many days of annual leave (vacation time) did you take last year? _____

29. Are you paid for unused annual leave (vacation time) at the end of each year?   (1) Yes   (2) No

IV. EDUCATIONAL BACKGROUND

30. Have you ever attended a community college?   (1) Yes (Answer question 30a.)   (2) No (Skip to question 31.)

     30a. If yes, did you earn an associate's degree?   (1) Yes   (2) No

31. Highest educational level attained:
    (1) Bachelor's degree   (2) Master's degree   (3) Ed. D.
    (4) Ph. D.   (5) Professional degree (MD, JD, DDS)   (8) Other (specify): _____

32. Major field of study in your highest degree: _____

33. Major field of study in your master's degree: _____

V. FAMILY INFORMATION

34. Father's most recent full-time occupation, even if deceased: Please be as specific as you can.
    _____

35. Highest educational level attained by your father:
    (1) Less than a high school diploma   (2) High school diploma   (3) Associate's   (4) Bachelor's
    (5) Master's   (6) Doctorate   (7) Other: _____

36. Mother's most recent full-time occupation, including homemaker, even if deceased: Please be as specific as you can.
    _____

37. Highest educational level attained by your mother:
    (1) Less than a high school diploma   (2) High school diploma   (3) Associate's   (4) Bachelor's
    (5) Master's   (6) Doctorate   (7) Other: _____

38. Age of spouse at last birthday: _____

39. Highest educational level attained by your spouse:
    (1) High school diploma   (2) Postsecondary proprietary diploma/degree   (3) Associate's degree
    (4) Bachelor's degree   (5) Master's degree   (6) Ed. D.
    (7) Ph. D.   (8) Professional degree (MD, JD, DDS)   (9) Other: _____

40. Does your spouse currently work outside the home for pay?
    (1) Yes, full-time (Answer question 40a.)   (2) Yes, part-time (Answer question 40a.)
    (3) No, spouse does not work outside the home for pay (Skip to question 41.)

    40a. If your spouse works outside the home, specify occupation: _____

VI. LIFESTYLE INFORMATION

41. Do you now live in the state in which you finished high school?   (1) Yes   (2) No

42. Do you have a commuter marriage?   (1) Yes (Answer questions 42a - 42c.)   (2) No (Skip to question 43.)

    42a. If you have a commuter marriage, who is the commuter? (1) I commute.   (2) Spouse commutes.

    42b. How far is the one-way commute?   (1) Up to 100 miles   (2) 101-250 miles
         (3) 250-1000 miles   (4) More than 1000 miles

    42c. How frequently does the commuter commute?   (1) Daily   (2) Weekly   (3) Other: _____

43. To which of the following organizations do you belong?
    (1) BPW   (2) Jaycees   (3) Junior League   (4) Kiwanis
    (5) League of Women Voters   (6) Lions   (7) Masons   (8) Rotary
    (9) Ruritan   (10) Social sorority   (11) Woman's forum   (12) Other: _____

44. Do you belong to a country club?   (1) Yes (Answer question 44a.)   (2) No (Skip to question 45.)

    44a. If yes, do you use it for professional entertaining?   (1) Yes   (2) No

45. Time permitting, in which of the following sports or activities do you participate on a regular basis?
    (1) Bowling   (2) Fishing   (3) Golf   (4) Hunting
    (5) Jogging   (6) Skiing   (7) Swimming   (8) Tennis
    (9) Aerobic exercise (other than those listed)   (10) Other_____

46. Circle the friends you see socially at least one hour per week outside of work.
    (1) Childhood friends   (2) Church associates   (3) Club associates   (4) Neighbors
    (5) Professional colleagues   (6) None   (7) Other: _____

47. If married, circle the friends your spouse sees socially at least one hour per week outside of work.
    (1) Childhood friends   (2) Church associates   (3) Club associates   (4) Neighbors
    (5) Professional colleagues   (6) None   (7) Other: _____

48. Did you take a vacation last year that lasted two weeks or more?
    (1) Yes (Answer question 48a.)   (2) No (Skip to question 49.)

    48a. Did you do any work related to your duties as president while on vacation?   (1) Yes   (2) No

VII. DEMOGRAPHIC INFORMATION

49. Age at last birthday: _____

50. Gender: (1) Male   (2) Female

51. Current marital status:
    (1) 1st marriage   (2) 2nd marriage   (3) 3rd marriage   (4) Separated   (5) Divorced—not remarried
    (6) Spouse deceased (not remarried)   (7) Not married—domestic partnership   (8) Single—never married

52. Race/ethnicity:
    (1) American Indian/Native American   (2) Asian-American/Pacific Islander
    (3) African American   (4) Hispanic
    (5) White/Caucasian   (6) Other _____

53. What is your religious affiliation?
    (1) Baptist   (2) Catholic   (3) Episcopalian
    (4) Jewish   (5) Lutheran   (6) Methodist
    (7) Muslim   (8) Presbyterian   (9) Other Protestant
    (10) None   (11) Other _____

54. What is your political party preference?   (1) Democrat   (2) Independent   (3) Republican   (4) Other _____

55. What is your political ideology?   (1) Liberal   (2) Moderate   (3) Conservative   (4) Other _____

IN YOUR OWN WORDS: (If more space is needed, please attach your comments.)
(1) Briefly identify what you see as the major issue facing the community college in the next 3 to 4 years.

(2) What you can do as president to prepare your institution to face the issue?

THANK YOU VERY MUCH FOR YOUR COOPERATION.

Appendix 2
Interview Questions

1. On the survey, presidents were asked to identify the most critical issue facing the community college in the next few years. At the top of the list was a lack of resources required to accomplish the college's mission. Do you agree that your community college does not have adequate resources to fulfill its mission?

   If yes, how has the college's mission been altered as a result of inadequate resources? What steps have you taken to obtain additional resources? If no, what have you done as president to assure that your college has adequate resources to fulfill its mission?

   What other outside influences are encroaching upon the college's ability to accomplish its mission, and indeed, to function effectively on a daily basis?

   How are you balancing the pressures of these influences with those of the college's mission?

2. More than 85 percent of the current community college presidents are Caucasian and approximately 82 percent are male. Do you feel that community college leaders should exert more effort to prepare and recruit minority (defined as non-Caucasian) and female presidents?

   If yes, what role do current presidents play in preparing future presidents? What are you doing to prepare minorities and women for the presidency?

   If no, why do you feel that more minority and women presidents are not needed?

3. Perhaps the most compelling development in American higher education in this half of the 20th century has been

the nation's commitment to open access. At the heart (and in many ways the soul) of the open access movement has been and are the community colleges. How do you define open access?

Do you feel that open access is threatened? If so, what are the threats?

4. Nearly 45 percent of the presidents stated that they plan to retire within the next six years. Imagine that you were contacted by a board from a community college in another state for assistance in developing its selection criteria for a new president. What skills or traits do you feel will be most important for the community college president in the 21st century?

What advice would you give to faculty in higher education graduate programs about the educational needs of tomorrow's presidents?

5. Do you have other comments about the current status of the presidency?

REFERENCES

Birnbaum, R. R. (1992). *How academic leadership works: Under-standing success and failure in the college presidency.* San Francisco: Jossey-Bass.

Blackwell, J. E. (1988, Summer). Faculty issues: The impact on minorities. *The Review of Higher Education, 11*(4), 417-434.

Boggs, G. R. (1988, April 30). Pathways to the presidency. Paper presented at the annual convention of the American Association of Community and Junior Colleges, Washington, D.C.

Burke, R. P. and Tolle, D. J. (1972). *The community college president at the turn of a new decade: The 1970s.* Unpublished manuscript.

Capozzoli, M. (1989). *A survey of women community college administrators.* (Technical Report No. 143). Princeton, NJ: Mid-Career Fellowship Program.

Carter, D. J. (1994, Fall). The status of faculty in community colleges: What do we know? In A. M. Cohen & F. B. Brawer (Series Eds.) & W. B. Harvey & J. Valadez, (Vol. Eds.), *New Directions for Community Colleges: No. 87, Creating and Maintaining a Diverse Faculty XXII*(3). (pp. 3-18). San Francisco: Jossey-Bass.

Carver, J. & Mayhew, M. (1994). *A new vision of board leadership: Governing the community college.* Washington, DC: Association of Community College Trustees.

Cohen, A. M. & Brawer, F. B. (1996). *The American community college: third edition.* San Francisco: Jossey-Bass.

Crowley, J. N. (1994). *No equal in the world: An interpretation of the academic presidency.* Reno: University of Nevada Press.

Department of Commerce. (1996). *Statistical abstract of the United States 1996: The national data book.* Washington, D.C.: United States Department of Commerce.

DiCroce, D. M. (1995, Spring). Women and the community college presidency: Challenges and possibilities. In A. M. Cohen & F. B. Brawer (Series Eds.) & B. K. Townsend (Vol. Ed.), *New Directions for Community Colleges: No. 89, Gender and Power in the Community College, XXIII*(1) (pp. 79-88). San Francisco: Jossey-Bass.

Eaton, J. S. (1984, Summer). Tapping neglected leadership sources. In A. M. Cohen & F. B. Brawer (Series Eds.) & R. L. Alfred, P. A. Elsner, R. J. LeCroy, N. Armes, (Vol. Eds.), *New Directions for Community Colleges: No. 46. Emerging Roles for Community College Leaders, XII*(2) (pp. 93-99). San Francisco: Jossey-Bass.

Fanelli, S. A. (1997, Summer). When a crisis occurs: A president's perspective. In A. M. Cohen & F. B. Brawer (Series Eds.) & I. M. Weisman & G. B. Vaughan, (Vol. Eds.), *New Directions for Community Colleges: No. 98, Presidents and Trustees in Partnership: New Roles and Leadership Challenges XXV*(2). (pp. 63-72). San Francisco: Jossey-Bass.

Fisher, J. (1991). *The board and the president.* Washington, D.C.: American Council on Education.

Gillett-Karam, R., Roueche, S. D., & Roueche, J. E. (1991). *Underrepresentation and the question of diversity: Women and minorities in the community college.* Washington, DC: Community College Press.

Healy, P. (1997, August, 15). The widely predicted growth in enrollment hasn't materialized in some states. *The Chronicle of Higher Education, XLIII* (49), pp. A23-A24.

Hughes, R. M. (1945). *A manual for trustees of colleges and universities.* Ames, IA: Iowa State College Press.

Kauffman, J. F. (1980). *At the pleasure of the board.* Washington, D. C.: American Council on Education.

Keeton, M. (1977). The constituencies and their claims. In G. L. Riley & J. V. Baldridge (Eds.), *Governing academic organizations: New problems, new perspectives* (pp. 194-210). Berkeley, CA: McCutchan Publishing Corporation.

Kerr, C. & Gade, M. L. (1989). *The guardians: Boards of trustees and American colleges and universities.* Washington, DC: Association of Governing Boards of Universities and Colleges.

Laden, B. V. (1996, Fall). The role of the professional associations in developing academic and administrative leaders. In A. M. Cohen & F. B. Brawer (Series Eds.) & J. C. Palmer & S. G. Katsinas, (Vol. Eds.), *New Directions for Community Colleges: No. 95, Graduate* and *Continuing Education for Community College Leaders XXIV*(3). (pp. 47-58). San Francisco: Jossey-Bass.

Lumsden, D. B., & Stewart, G. B. (1992, Spring). American colleges and universities offering course work on two-year institutions: Results of a national survey. *Community College Review (19)*4, 34 46.

Nason, J. W. (1982). *The nature of trusteeship: The role and responsibilities of college and university boards.* Washington, D.C.: Association of Governing Boards of Universities and Colleges.

Phelps, D. G., & Taber, L. S. (1996, summer). Affirmative action as an equal opportunity opportunity. In A. M. Cohen & F. B. Brawer (Series Eds.) & R. C. Bowen & G. H. Muller, (Vol. Eds.), *New Directions for Community Colleges: No. 94, Achieving Administrative Diversity XXIV*(2). (pp. 67-80). San Francisco: Jossey-Bass.

Pierce, D. R., Mahoney, J. R., & Kee, A. M. (1996, Summer). Professional development resources for minority administrators. In A. M. Cohen & F. B. Brawer (Series Eds.) & R. C. Bowen & G. H. Muller, (Vol. Eds.), *New Directions for Community Colleges: No. 94, Achieving Administrative Diversity XXIV*(2). (pp. 81-92). San Francisco: Jossey-Bass.

Pray, F. C. (1975). *A new look at community college boards of trustees and presidents and their relationships: Suggestions for change.* Washington, D.C.: American Association of Community and Junior Colleges.

Rauh, M. A. (1969). *The trusteeship of colleges and universities.* New York: McGraw-Hill.

Rendon, L. I., & Valadez, J. R. (1994). New wave students and the community college. In G. A. Baker, III (Ed.), *A handbook on the community college in America: Its history* (pp. 565-579). Westport, CT: Greenwood Press.

Riche, M. F. (1996). *How America is changing—the view from the Census Bureau, 1995.* In R. Famighetti (Ed.), The World Almanac and Book of Facts 1996, p 382-445. Mahwah, NJ: Funk & Wagnalls Corporation.

Rucker, T. (1997, June 29). Alabama board proposes $102 million in ed. cuts. *Community College Times, IX* (15), pp. 2-3.

Schultz, R. E. (1965, October). Changing profile of the junior college president. *Junior College Journal, (36),* pp. 8-13.

Sullivan, L. G. (1997). I'm their leader: Which way did they go? *Journal of the American Association for Women in Community Colleges,* pp. 12-17.

Townsend, B. K. (1996, Fall). The role of the professoriate in influencing future community college leadership. In A. M. Cohen & F. B.

Brawer (Series Eds.) & J. C. Palmer & S. G. Katsinas (Vol. Eds.), *New Directions for Community Colleges: No. 95, Graduate and Continuing Education for Community College Leaders: What It Means Today, XXIV*(3) (pp. 59-64). San Francisco: Jossey-Bass.

Twombly, S. B. (1995, Spring). Gendered images of community college leadership: What messages they send. In A. M. Cohen & F. B. Brawer (Series Eds.) & B. K. Townsend (Vol. Ed.), *New Directions for Community Colleges: No. 89, Gender and Power in the Community College, XXIII*(1) (pp. 67-78). San Francisco: Jossey-Bass.

Vaughan, G. B. (1986). *The community college presidency.* New York: American Council on Education/MacMillan.

Vaughan, G. B. (1989). *Leadership in transition: The community college presidency.* New York: American Council on Education/MacMillan.

Vaughan, G. B. (1990). *Pathway to the presidency: Community college deans of instruction.* Washington, D. C.: Community College Press.

Vaughan, G. B. (1994) Effective presidential leadership: Twelve areas of focus. In A. M. Cohen, Florence B. Brawer, & Associates, *Managing Community Colleges: A Handbook for Effective Practice.* San Francisco: Jossey-Bass.

Vaughan, G. B. (1996, Summer). Paradox and promise: Leadership and the neglected minorities. In A. M. Cohen & F. B. Brawer (Series Eds.) & R. C. Bowen & G. H. Muller, (Vol. Eds.), *New Directions for Community Colleges: No. 94, Achieving Administrative Diversity XXIV*(2). (pp. 5-12). San Francisco: Jossey-Bass.

Vaughan, G. B., Mellander, G. A., & Blois, B. (1994). *The community college presidency: Current status and future outlook.* Washington, DC: American Association of Community Colleges.

Vaughan, G. B., & Weisman, I. M. (1997). *Community college trustees: Leading on behalf of their communities.* Washington, DC: Association of Community College Trustees.

Whitmore, L. A. (1987). *A national study of local community college trustees.* (Doctoral dissertation, University of Texas at Austin, 1987). *Dissertation Abstracts International 49-03A*, 403.

Widmer, C. (1987, October/December). Minority participation on boards of directors of human service agencies: some evidence and suggestions. *Journal of Voluntary Action Research 16*(4), 33-44.

Wilson, R. (1996, Summer). The unfinished agenda. In A. M. Cohen & F. B. Brawer (Series Eds.) & R. C. Bowen & G. H. Muller (Vol. Eds.), *New Directions for Community Colleges: No. 94, Achieving Administrative Diversity, XXIV*(2) (pp. 93-100). San Francisco: Jossey-Bass.

INDEX

About the Authors

George B. Vaughan is a professor of higher education and editor of the *Community College Review* in the Department of Adult and Community College Education at North Carolina State University. Before becoming a professor, he served as a community college president for 17 years. He has written a number of books and articles on the community college, including *The Community College Presidency*. He received the 1996 National Leadership Award from the American Association of Community Colleges.

Iris M. Weisman is a visiting assistant professor with the Academy for Community College Leadership Advancement, Innovation, and Modeling (ACCLAIM) in the Department of Adult and Community College Education at North Carolina State University. She has 11 years of academic affairs and student services experience at Pima Community College in Tucson, Arizona.

The authors also collaborated on *Community College Trustees: Leading on Behalf of Their Communities* and *Presidents and Trustees in Partnership: New Roles and Leadership Challenges.*